This is a story about a dream that became a reality. As partners in marriage and life, Dallen and Glennis became partners in business. It is one of the great success stories of our time. There is a lot for us to learn from their life, their work, and their faith.

Bill Pollard, chairman and CEO of ServiceMaster

This is the story of a man who lives out his worldview—that God has placed us in the world for a purpose and that what we do has both an immediate and eternal impact. Guided by the truth of God's Word, Dallen discovered his purpose and balanced his work ethic with his faith, his entrepreneurial skill with his dependence on God. Dallen has found real success—doing what's right, loving and serving others, and walking humbly with God. Anyone who reads this book finds a remarkable and inspirational window into the life of a humble Christian who does God's work in the real world.

Joanne Kemp, wife of Jack Kemp, former congressman and secretary of HUD, currently codirector of Empower America

Dallen Peterson has been a real blessing in my life, not only as a political supporter but more important as a friend who nurtured my budding faith with his solid example of what it means to live as God's servant. Dallen has discovered what true riches are—not the riches of this world but the eternal riches of life in Christ. While Dallen is a wealthy man, you could take all of his money away tomorrow, and he would still be the same man—loving, committed, faithful, and true. This book will challenge you to have your priorities in the right investments, not the short-term investments in the here and now but the eternal investments in the hereafter.

Kay Orr, former state treasurer and governor of Nebraska

Rags,
Riches,
& Real
Success

Dallen Peterson
with Ellen Vaughn

Tyndale House Publishers, Inc.
Wheaton, Illinois

Visit Tyndale's exciting Web site at www.tyndale.com

Rags, Riches, and Real Success

Copyright © 2000 by Dallen Peterson. All rights reserved.

Cover photo copyright © 1999 by Stefan Adreev. All rights reserved.

Designed by Catherine Bergstrom

Edited by Lynn Vanderzalm

Library of Congress Cataloging-in-Publication Data

Peterson, Dallen.
    Rags, riches, and real success / by Dallen Peterson with Ellen Vaughn.
       p. cm.
    Includes bibliographical references.
    ISBN 0-8423-3956-6 (sc)
       1. ServiceMaster Company. 2. Building cleaning industry—United States—Management.
    3. New business enterprises—United States—Management. 4. Self-employed—United States.
    5. House cleaning—United States. I. Vaughn, Ellen Santilli. II. Title.
    HD9999.B884 S47 2000
    658—dc21   00-032529

Printed in the United States of America

05 04 03 02 01 00
 8   7   6   5   4   3   2   1

To Glennis

and

Kim, Kris, Brian, Karma, and Brett—

with love and thanks

Contents

Foreword

If you've picked up this book looking for a get-rich-quick formula or a seven-steps-to-success manual, you're in for a great surprise.

Yes, this is an exciting story about success and the American dream—but it is much, much more. Many of the truths and principles that emerge from these pages buck the tide of today's demand for instant gratification. In fact, some of them may be a little tough for you to swallow.

This book goes against the grain. That's what is so refreshing about it. It challenges and redefines what we think of as success and what it takes to achieve it. And more important, it also teaches us how to handle success.

Handling success may sound easy, but many people have succeeded financially only to lose everything else that is infinitely more valuable—their marriages, families, and friendships. Some people, in fact, can handle adversity much better than success.

That was the case for me. I achieved every professional goal I ever set. I climbed my way to the top, which for me was the office next to the president of the United States. I had position, prestige, and power. And I was miserable.

Paradoxically, it was in prison that I found peace. There, I learned the lessons my friend Dallen has sought to relate in this book.

So as you read, you're in for a challenge—and a treat. You're going to meet a man I've come to love and respect enormously. Dallen Peterson has been a friend for twenty-five years now, and as you'll see by his refreshing candor, he'd be the first to say he's an ordinary guy. His roots—and values—go deep in the midwestern soil on which he grew up. He served in the military, married young, and struggled to make ends meet as his family grew while he finished college. He's gone through his share of challenges, failures, and successes—and then, through hard work, a big vision, and a lot of faith, he achieved stunning business success that has multiplied over the years into great wealth.

I first met Dallen in 1976, when I was speaking at a city-wide prayer breakfast in Omaha, Nebraska. Back then people were very curious about my Watergate past, my prison experience, and my conversion to Christ, and I was invited to speak all over the country. I met thousands of people. But Dallen left a lasting impression, both because of his infectious enthusiasm and because of his compassion for the downtrodden. We shared a commitment to men and women in prison, and our friendship grew.

So I knew Dallen back when he risked everything and started Merry Maids, when he was cleaning floors and scrubbing toilets. And I've known Dallen as he's achieved fabulous business success.

For me the most endearing quality about Dallen is that he's exactly the same person as a hugely successful entrepreneur that he was when he washed floors on his knees with his fellow workers.

And therein lies one of the richest lessons to be learned from this wonderfully engaging story.

What impresses me most about Dallen and his wonderful wife, Glennis—who keeps him in line, much the way Patty does me—is not what they did to make a big pile of money. Lots of people do that. What impresses me is what they *did* when they made their money.

Lots of get-rich books that fill the bookstore shelves never ask the important questions Dallen and Glennis asked: What do you do when you achieve success in any area of life? What do you do after you realize your dream? In that, Dallen and Glennis's story is unique, an example to us all.

When they hit the jackpot, they didn't accumulate a lot of fancy toys or plunge into a flashy lifestyle (or split up, which is often the case).

No, they went back to Sunburg, Minnesota, built a home a few hundred yards from the family homestead where Dallen was born, and settled down to spend time with their children and grandchildren. Their five kids and nineteen grandchildren (at this count) are a testimony to their love and commitment.

And their friends in nearby New London (population 791), where Dallen goes to have "coffee with the boys" every morning, will tell you that Dallen and Glennis are the same people they've always been. They're truly interested in others. They'll help anyone in need. They don't take themselves too seriously. They laugh a lot. And they're hard workers, whatever they take on.

In today's transient culture they understand the importance of the roots of family, friends, and faith. No matter how well or poorly things have gone, they've kept life's essential priorities straight.

A few paragraphs ago I said that Dallen is the same person today that he was when I met him in 1976. But that's not exactly correct.

Even before we met, Dallen had been working in the prisons. He had few resources in those days, but he had a big heart for the needy and hopeless. As you'll read, he and Glennis had opened their home to the homeless. When a kid they knew got in trouble, they visited him in prison right away. Then they started a Bible study for him and his friends, a study that continued for twelve years and introduced dozens of inmates to a new life and a fresh perspective.

After Dallen and I met, he became a volunteer leader for Prison Fellowship. Shortly after he sold Merry Maids, I invited him to serve on our board of directors. And what I've seen is that the more success he's had, the more he's grown to care for those in need. He's visited some of the country's toughest prisons with me—in fact, we've celebrated eight Easter Sundays together with men behind bars. Most people enjoy Easter in the comfort of their home church with a big brunch afterward. Not Dallen. He has learned that life's real joy and success come not in gratifying oneself but in helping others.

I've come to appreciate Dallen's wisdom as well. We've had to confront some tough decisions along the way as Prison Fellowship has grown from a handful of us back in 1976 to a movement of fifty thousand volunteers and a staff of four hundred. Dallen's insights have been invaluable. In fact, it was

Dallen's vision and courage that broke an impasse on our board and led to the founding of America's first Christian prison: InnerChange Freedom Initiative in Houston, Texas.

So I've seen the principles you'll read about in this book up close, as my friend Dallen has lived them. They're true!

I hope you'll enjoy this refreshing book. I promise you that if you invest the time it will take to read it—an evening or two—you will reap great benefits, and not just in terms of learning the steps to business success, valuable as that is. No, you'll learn the far deeper principles of success in life itself, whatever your endeavor, the real success that brings not just prosperity but also reconciled relationships, help to others, and a lasting sense of peace and purpose.

Charles W. Colson
Washington, D.C.

Part One
My Story

Unlikely Beginnings

I shivered in the brisk Nebraska wind as I left for work that winter day more than twenty years ago. Instead of my usual suit and tie, I wore a pair of jeans and a denim shirt. Instead of my gleaming leather briefcase, I carried a scrub brush and a bucket. And instead of my former executive-office colleagues, I had a new business partner and two new employees: my wife, Glennis, and the youngest of our five children, Karma and Brett.

It was December 27, 1979. I grinned at Glennis—it was her birthday, after all—as we arrived at the home of our very first customer. Starting a maid-service company was an idea I had researched carefully, but I also had a strong gut feeling that our new business was going to be a winner. I could barely contain my excitement. Glennis and the kids were a little more dubious, but they were humoring me.

We had run a three-line ad in our local Omaha newspaper the day before, and our first call had come from a realtor who needed a house cleaned before it could be put on the market. The house was very small, she said, just a kitchen, bedroom, living room, and bath. It didn't sound like that would take

much work; I calculated quickly in my head and quoted her
a fee of $66.

The realtor had given us a key. Whistling, I fitted it into
the lock and swung open the old front door. The grin faded
from my face, and behind me Glennis and the kids first
groaned, then laughed, then groaned again.

Newspapers, magazines, and trash towered in piles all
over the living-room carpet. The windows were so coated
with grime that no light filtered through them. As we gin-
gerly stepped inside, we saw that the kitchen cabinets, floors,
and appliances were so layered with dirt and grease that we
couldn't even tell what color they were. The whole house
stank, and my heart sank.

"Well," Glennis said, trying to look on the bright side
even though there was absolutely nothing bright in the mess
in front of us, "I guess we'll just have to dig right in!"

"Right," I said. "I'm going home."

She looked at me sharply, as if I were deserting her.

"I'll be right back," I assured her. "I'm just going to get
some snow scoops to shovel out this place."

The four of us spent the whole first day just in the kitchen.
That night, as we stumbled back to our car, we looked like
wrung-out dishrags.

Driving home, I looked at Glennis. "Well, have you ever
had a better birthday?"

She didn't laugh.

The next day, we went back to our house of horrors and
continued to scrape and scrub and polish and vacuum. By the
end of the day, that little home shone, and we were absolutely
bedraggled. I slumped at my desk and added up the time the

four of us had put into that place: a total of sixty-six work hours. At the rate I'd quoted over the phone, we'd earned exactly a dollar an hour.

Not exactly an auspicious beginning for Merry Maids.

But less than eight years after that winter day, Glennis and I sold our Merry Maids business for $25 million. And today, Merry Maids is the largest homecleaning company in the world. We have 1,275 franchises in all fifty states and in eleven foreign countries, employing eighty-five hundred people. Our consumer level of revenue will exceed $275 million this year.

But the Merry Maids story isn't just one of business success. It's a story about deeper, lasting success in people's lives—from people in prison cells to those in the governor's mansion and everywhere in between. And it's a story that shows that the American dream is alive and well, that high hopes can still be realized through hard work and dogged determination.

And at its heart the Merry Maids story is about the source of all hope: the God who loves us all intimately and whose good plans for us often come true in the most surprising, unlikely ways.

That's where my story begins: on a November day in 1936, on a small Minnesota farm, when my mother prepared to give birth to her firstborn son—and, much to her surprise, delivered not one, but two.

Roots

It was near the end of 1936. Franklin Roosevelt had just won his landslide reelection to a second term as president of the United States. A few months earlier, Jesse Owens had won four gold medals at the Berlin Olympics, much to the fury of Germany's chancellor, Adolf Hitler. And as Mussolini's Italy annexed Ethiopia and Nazi troops invaded the Rhineland, the clouds of World War II had begun to gather.

But all that was far away from Sunburg, Minnesota, where a young woman named Melvina Peterson was anticipating the birth of her first child, due at Christmas. She and my father, Walter, had been married for two years. They lived on the rich Minnesota farmland that had first been settled by my great-grandfather, Nels Peterson.

When he arrived from Norway in 1859, looking for a future full of promise, Nels sank his hardy roots deep in American soil. And so the peaceful land in the middle of Minnesota became home to a long line of plainspoken, God-fearing, hardworking Petersons, whose lives moved rhythmically from season to season, through planting, cultivation, harvest, and rest. And snow. There was always a lot of snow in the central Minnesota farm country.

On the morning of November 18, my father drove my mother to Willmar, the small town twenty miles away from their farm in Sunburg, to buy some baby clothes. Chatting with the clerk in the small country store, she bought little shirts, diapers, and a warm, white blanket. Then she made the journey back to the snug brick farmhouse on the hill.

Later that afternoon my mother and a friend were making lefse, the traditional Norwegian pastry served during the Christmas season. My mother stood in the warm farmhouse kitchen, a floury apron wrapped around her ample middle, vigorously rolling out the fragile, white dough. Snowflakes gently drifted past the steamy kitchen windows.

Mom began to feel labor pains. She kept rolling dough. The pains kept coming. She reluctantly put aside her work, made a few phone calls, and retired to the cozy first-floor bedroom that she and my father shared.

Mom's mother arrived. The doctor arrived. The pains kept coming. My mother, a durable young woman who was not easily agitated, calmly delivered her firstborn, a healthy baby boy. My grandmother, a bit more nervous, shakily wrapped the howling new baby in a clean blanket. The doctor bent down, reassessed the situation, and announced to my mother, "All right, Mrs. Peterson, we'll need to keep going here. There's another one!"

My mother told me later, in her lilting Norwegian accent, "I was young and strong. I didn't worry about anything. I thought it was exciting."

My grandmother, on the other hand, clutched her hand

to her chest, moaned once, and slumped to the floor. "Wait just a moment, Mrs. Peterson," said the doctor. "Let me give your mother a little medication."

Forty-five minutes later, I was born.

■ ■ ■

My identical twin brother, Dale, and I were eventually joined over the years by seven more siblings. Life on our family farm in those early days set the patterns that would remain with me all of my life: hard work, easy laughter, and the firm foundations of faith, family, and friends.

Our farmhouse sat on a hill overlooking woods, pastures, cornfields, and the gentle slope down to the sparkling waters of Norway Lake. My father raised corn, soybeans, and beef cattle; he put in roads and started a sawmill business. When Dale and I were about six years old, I remember bumpily driving the tractor down the straight rows of the hayfield, one of us steering, the other managing the clutch, our blond hair blowing in the breeze. We climbed trees, swam, skated on the lake, tossed basketballs, and performed creative experiments on chickens. Life on the farm was very good, and although we worked hard, we played hard too.

When I was about three years old, my father took the family car down to the lake one afternoon to wash it. Dale and I—always together, always dressed alike—tagged along. We played at the water's edge while Dad sudsed down the old Ford. Some time before, hunters had set up a duck blind of sorts, immersing large wooden crates deep into the soft muck at the water's edge, hiding them behind the high grasses.

As Dale and I rambled along, throwing rocks into the lake

and splashing in the shallow water, I stumbled into one of the wooden crates. I tumbled headfirst into the water and became trapped in the old box, and in the process I gave Dale his first vivid memory. Seeing me floating facedown, not moving, he jumped in and tried to pull me up. But I was deadweight, the same size as he was, and he couldn't do it. Dale screamed for my father, who ran to the water's edge and hauled me out.

I wasn't breathing. Dad forced the water out of my lungs and his own air into me. I coughed, sputtered, and came back. Dad didn't tell my mother about the incident until about twenty years later, when he was fairly sure she wouldn't kill him.

But such moments of drama were few, and as I look back, I recognize it as a healthy, happy, and very provincial upbringing. Our community was primarily Norwegian, all Lutheran. I didn't even meet a person of another faith until high school. We never missed church on Sundays, and my father made sure we all kept the Sabbath as a day of rest. The church was the center of our social lives.

Yet we didn't talk much about Christianity. My parents lived their faith without question. But they, like everyone else I knew, considered religious faith to be a private matter, and it was not something we discussed.

So, in those early days, everyone I knew was of the same ethnic and religious background. Everyone I knew was involved in farming. Everyone I knew seemed content. And so was I.

But still, there was a small spark of something like restlessness within me. One day, when I was about twelve years old, I remember sitting in the kitchen, thumbing through a *Time* magazine. On one page was an advertisement, a picture of a well-dressed businessman carrying a briefcase. I didn't know who that man was or where he was going, but I stared at that ad for a long time. Then I looked out the sparkling windows of my mother's clean kitchen, toward the endless rows of corn-fields stretching as far as I could see.

When I grow up, I thought, *I want to be the man with the brief-case.*

CHAPTER 3

The Man with
the Briefcase

Dale and I attended a small country school in District 13, about
three miles from our home. We'd walk the distance unless it
was really cold; then Dad would drive us in his old Ford. It was
a classic country one-room schoolhouse, with a grand total of
thirty students. My eighth-grade class consisted of four kids:
two girls, named Phyllis and Inez, and Dale and me.

So, as you can imagine, our social life was pretty simple—
holiday celebrations, ice-cream socials, relatives, school friends,
and church. Our lives were isolated to our little corner of
Minnesota; we knew very little of the outside world, and we
preferred it that way.

But when Dale and I were seniors in high school, we
expanded our experience by joining the army reserves. After
we graduated in 1954, we were shipped off to basic training at
Camp McCoy in Wisconsin.

Glennis and I were already engaged by then; we had met
early on in high school and had been pretty serious about our
intentions from the very beginning. By the time I left for basic
training, Glennis had developed rheumatic fever and had been

hospitalized most of the summer. The illness left her very weak, and I tried to be with her as much as possible. Looking back, that was just about the only time in our lives together that I've seen Glennis physically incapacitated. Otherwise she has been absolutely tireless, whether we were having children, starting a new business, playing golf or water-skiing, or just about anything else!

Dale and I went on active duty in the army in December 1954. Glennis and I married in March 1955 and spent two years in California, where our daughter Kim was born.

After leaving the army, I enrolled in the University of Minnesota. Glennis and I lived in student housing; our only income was $160 a month from the GI Bill. Glennis baby-sat for an additional $10 a week. Out of this princely sum we had to pay for tuition, books, rent, food, clothes, and diapers, since we had two children, Kim and Kris, by the time I got out of college.

I've never forgotten those days when we had to budget every penny—and when buying just a half gallon of ice cream was a special luxury.

I majored in agriculture education, with a minor in business. I was interested in the food industry, and when I graduated in 1960, I took an accounting position with Fairmont Foods, a dairy and snack-food company in Minneapolis. My starting pay was $300 a month. After six months I got a surprise $50 raise. Glennis and I felt as if we had won the lottery—we had never experienced so much money in our lives!

I was fortunate to work for a wonderful man, Everett Redfield. He took me under his wing and taught me little principles about life and business—principles that you can learn only in a mentoring relationship. We would work late, and then he would take me out to dinner. He invested time in our relationship, and through Everett I learned how to do the same for others. His model of mentoring became my own over the years that followed.

Everett taught me well, and my rise at Fairmont was rather rapid. I transferred from my first branch in Minneapolis to St. Paul in 1963 and became the controller of their new snack-foods operation. I then was promoted to be the plant manager, and in 1965 I moved to Centralia, Illinois, and then in 1967 to Terre Haute, Indiana, to manage a plant of more than five hundred employees.

The Terre Haute plant had had three union walkouts, and labor relations with management were in serious peril. The plant personnel just did not trust management.

From that situation I learned an important principle: line workers, just like service workers anywhere, are very perceptive! They can immediately sense whether or not you are a person of integrity. Because I focused on relationships, as I'll discuss in chapter 13, things smoothed out quite a bit. Within a year that plant became the most profitable producer in the snack-foods division of Fairmont Foods.

In the summer of 1969 I became manager of the snack-foods division, and that promotion led to our move to Omaha, Nebraska. Soon I became the division vice president—and by this point, I was not only the man with the briefcase but also the man who traveled forty-eight weeks a year.

I would leave home on Monday mornings; Glennis would cry as she dropped me off at the airport. I would return at the end of the week, sometimes on Thursday night, but more often on Friday. I was rising in the corporate ranks and seeing that the higher up the totem pole you were climbing, the greasier the pole became.

I was thirty-three years old, with two thousand employees in my division, one wife, and five children—Kim, thirteen; Kris, twelve; Brian, ten; Karma, eight; and Brett, two. I loved my work and I loved my family—but Glennis was shouldering a very heavy burden, which I, in my usual cheerful way, largely ignored. For me, like many executives, career success and the financial rewards it afforded me were taking me away from my first love, the family I was working so hard to support.

I was highly motivated to succeed, driven to be the best that I could be in the workplace. I thought that the best way to do that was to spend long hours on the road and in the office. Today I realize that more time invested in the work does not necessarily equate to greater productivity or performance. I could have delegated more, surrounded myself with people more insightful than I, people who could better manage the workload. In short, I could have worked smarter, not harder.

But back then I was caught in the whirlwind of it all, even as I began to wonder if this was all there was. When I looked at executives who had been in their positions longer than I had been in mine, I realized I didn't really want their lifestyle. I couldn't really foresee a future much different from the present, unless I waited until retirement. I was as busy as ever, but each Monday morning, as I got off a plane in some remote airport that looked like every other airport, I felt tired and hollow inside.

I sometimes wonder what might have happened if

Glennis and I had not attended a retreat on Labor Day weekend, 1969. . . .

Soon after moving to Omaha, we visited various local Lutheran churches. After all, wherever we lived, we always went to church: it was an unquestioned part of our culture. We were impressed with the friendly people of Calvary Lutheran. They welcomed us into their fellowship, so we began to put down our roots there.

But when Glennis suggested that we attend a three-day family retreat on Labor Day weekend, I was resistant. After a hard week on the road, I wanted to relax and play golf! "All right," I told Glennis. "We'll go to the retreat just for the day, but we won't spend the night." I wanted the opportunity to escape if it was dull.

The retreat wasn't dull. I was so impressed with the people: their joy, and love, and their knowledge of the Bible. I had never been around Christians who expressed their faith with such vitality and intimacy, and although that openness repelled me ever so slightly—after all, wasn't faith supposed to be a *private* matter?—it also compelled me.

Driving home after the first session, I told Glennis, "Let's go back tomorrow." We did, and then on the following day as well. Glennis knew that something strange was happening for me to give up my golf game for the entire weekend.

I hadn't known that I was spiritually searching, but the fellowship with the Christians in that church and the teaching from the pastor, Bob Ellison, began to strike a chord that I never knew existed in me. Glennis felt the same way, and as the weeks went by, we became more and more involved with Calvary Lutheran Church.

Typically, we jumped right in, just a little bit over our heads. We weren't at the church long before Bob Ellison and some new friends, Dick and Ireta Kerns, talked us into signing up for Evangelism Explosion, a training program for people to share their faith with others. Glennis and I didn't even realize that *we* did not yet understand the gospel at that point. But we would soon find out.

One night we were sitting in the training meeting, looking at one of the key questions in the material: "If you were to die tonight, what assurance would you have of going to heaven?" That caught me off guard. I had always thought that I was pretty good: I had always gone to church and helped people in need. But now, as I thought about it, I realized I had no assurance of going to heaven. I realized I couldn't be "good" enough to meet God's standard: absolute moral perfection. I realized that trusting in Christ was my only hope. And so, without much drama or fanfare, I prayed to receive Christ.

For Glennis the journey was similar. She was at home one morning, sewing, thinking about what we had learned. She realized that she, like me, had never actually committed her life to Christ. She quietly prayed and did so.

But then she had a problem: she remembered from our training that it's good to tell someone right away, so you have a witness, so to speak, of your decision. I was traveling, the older kids were in school, and Glennis thought that Brett, our two-year-old, probably didn't count.

She kept sewing. *I don't have to tell anyone,* she thought. *Yes, you do,* came into her mind. *I don't want to,* she argued. This went on for hours. Finally Glennis threw down her sewing, went to the phone, and called Ireta Kerns.

Dick answered the phone. "Ireta's not here," he told Glennis. "She'll be back in about fifteen minutes."

"I can't wait that long!" Glennis burst out. "That's too late!"

"What is it?" asked Dick, alarmed. It wasn't like Glennis to sound so urgent or emotional.

"I accepted Christ!" Glennis cried into the phone, bursting into tears.

Meanwhile I bought a small New Testament that fit easily into my briefcase. I read it within ten days. I would sit on airplanes and devour the Scriptures, hungry in a new way to understand the compelling character of this man called Jesus Christ.

On the outside I didn't appear to be very different: I was still a nice person, an affable man who cared for others. But inside, I had a new sense of purpose and excitement, fueled by the simple knowledge that I knew I was saved.

Today that type of plain language doesn't connect with a lot of people in the business world: being "saved" sounds so backwoods, so outmoded, so simplistic. But I will never forget the incredible sense of liberation I felt. I was free, forgiven of the muck inside of me, assured of living forever in the presence of Christ! Faith wasn't an issue of good works or church attendance, as I had always assumed; it was a relationship with Jesus.

I've never shied away from being very clear about my Christian commitment. At the same time, I've tried not to trample on other people's different religious beliefs—or lack of them. I believe that the most profound witness of Christian faith comes through demonstration, not articulation.

Particularly in today's cultural environment, people are drawn to Christ not so much through sermons or verbal persuasion as through seeing his love lived out through those who claim his name. And sadly, when Christians talk about our faith but don't live it, we fail miserably.

As the writer Sheldon Vanauken put it in *A Severe Mercy*, "The best argument for Christianity is Christians: their joy, their certainty, their completeness. But the strongest argument against Christianity is also Christians—when they are somber and joyless, when they are self-righteous and smug in complacent consecration, when they are narrow and repressive, then Christianity dies a thousand deaths."

At any rate, over the years I have sought—with varying degrees of success—to *live* my faith in the marketplace, more than I've talked about it.

Some people's life stories make it sound as if conversion is the end, that coming to Jesus means that life becomes neat and tidy and that we become healthy and wealthy. Glennis and I have certainly experienced great blessings, material and otherwise, but our Christian commitments in 1969 didn't simplify our lives.

No, things got a lot messier and a lot more complicated for us. Meeting Christ meant that we met a lot of other people too. The next thing I knew, Sophia the trapeze artist was living in our home, and I was on my way to prison.

CHAPTER 4

Nine
Bedrooms

As time went on, I continued my crazy traveling schedule with Fairmont, but now the weekends were full of church activities. Since Glennis and I had five children, two of whom were in high school, we threw ourselves into the church's programs for high-school kids. And then we got involved in a program called household ministry, an opportunity to open our home to people in need of a temporary place to live. The church elders provided oversight; the people who received housing had to agree to certain stipulations, like abiding by house rules, attending church, and staying away from drugs and alcohol.

Glennis and I already lived in a state of controlled chaos, with our children and their friends running in and out all the time. Why not add a few more? We decided to open our doors to people in need.

Our first houseguest was a boy whose father was a member of our church, but they had a substantial rift in their relationship, and the boy needed a place to live. Another was Bryan, a teenager from Memphis. Bryan's parents were divorced, and neither his mom nor his dad could handle him.

To us, Bryan was a polite kid with great manners, but he didn't want anyone touching him. Even if I put my hand on his arm, he'd instinctively flinch. One night soon after he arrived, one of our kids knocked over a glass of milk on the dinner table, and I watched as Bryan hunched over, his shoulders tense. It was clear that he was used to yelling, angry explosions, hitting—and those things didn't happen in our family.

It took about a year before he adjusted to being touched or hugged. He lived with us for three years; our Brian was the same age, and the two boys both ended up working part-time at McDonald's, splitting shifts.

As time went by, we thought that since we were expanding our family through this household ministry, we might as well expand our house. We found the perfect home: nine bedrooms, five bathrooms, three miles from church.

Over the years, dozens of people in need became part of our family. People like Bonnie, who had been living in her car; B. J., a South Dakota kid who called Glennis "Mudder"; a thirty-year-old, Bill, who had a job and a fairly stable life but just needed a place to stay for a while; and Sandy, a mentally handicapped young woman who arrived at our home with her six-week-old infant. She kept forgetting to feed the baby, and Glennis had to make sure that Sandy, in many ways a child herself, cared properly for her own child.

Then there was Linda, who called us from a pay phone one hot Sunday afternoon. I went to pick her up and found that she had been living in an old car with a toddler, a six-month-old child, and a dog.

I don't think Linda had ever set foot in a church until she came to live with us. But she committed her life to Christ after coming to Calvary Lutheran a few times, and she lived with us for months. Her boyfriend, Bryce, was eventually released from where he had been serving time in prison, and he and Linda were married at our church. I served as the official wedding photographer!

Like Linda, most people who came to live with us ended up becoming Christians. It seemed as if we spent half our time in church, with Sunday morning and evening services as well as an assortment of weeknight meetings.

And every morning we would start the day together at seven o'clock with family devotions. We all sat around the kitchen table, which had a four-by-eight-foot sheet of plywood over it to make it big enough for twelve people. Glennis or one of the older kids or I would lead a short Bible study, and then we would all hold hands and pray, committing our day to God. And then we would jump up and head out in at least twelve different directions.

Looking back, I'm not sure how we did it, but Glennis ran a tight ship. On Sundays we'd all come back from church to the aroma of a big roast cooking in the oven, and we'd sit down to roast beef, mashed potatoes, and gravy. There were mountains of dishes to be washed, heaps of laundry to sort, piles of socks to match, mounds of homework to help with—but it was a healthy, happy environment that gave a lot of kids who stayed with us something they had never before experienced: the security of a stable home headed by a husband and wife who loved each other and sought to love God. Glennis and I felt so blessed by the secure and loving homes we had grown up in that we wanted to pass those foundations of faith, family, and friends on to others.

The household ministry was also a tremendous, although sometimes difficult, learning experience for our children. Our daughter Kim says that she and her siblings were sometimes jealous of the attention I gave to the people who came to live with us. Our children would—not always affectionately—dub the newest household member "brother" or "sister," as in "Brother Bryan." When Glennis and I would take yet another less-than-attractive person under our wings, the kids would look on and say, "Yeah, that's great, but what about us?"

But today Kim says that our full house back then was precisely the reason she and the others were able to grow up with very open attitudes toward others. Although our children could have grown up with a rather insulated middle-class lifestyle, they were exposed early on to those who had suffered life's harsh realities, from homelessness to prison to fractured families.

As a result, our children learned not to judge people by outward appearances—like skin color, economic position, or ethnic background. They learned to value relationships with those who were different. That's one of life's most important lessons, which they are now passing on to their own children.

But it wasn't always easy!

After we moved to the big house, a young woman I'll call Sophia came to live with us. Originally from Hungary, Sophia, a petite and dark-haired woman, was in her late thirties. She was separated from her husband and worked as a circus performer. But her alcoholism had tended to interfere with her trapeze career, and she ended up living with us.

I had never been around an alcoholic before, and we were absolutely amazed by Sophia's resourcefulness when it came to obtaining and hiding her booze. We would find empty bottles stuffed in the laundry hamper, under the mattress, behind the commode. We hardly ever let Sophia out of our sight, and even when she went for a walk in the neighborhood, Glennis would usually have our daughter Kim go with her to make sure Sophia didn't get into trouble or head to the liquor store. I'll never know how she did it—she had hardly any money—but Sophia always found a way to support her habit.

One night Glennis and I were dead asleep, no doubt dreaming about laundry and snack foods and the other mundane elements of our busy lives, when there was a rap on our bedroom door.

"Dallen!" Sophia rasped in a hoarse whisper. "You've got to come out here!"

I came to life, thinking that one of the children was sick, and stumbled to the door.

Sophia's hair was sticking straight up all over her head, and her words were slurred. "You've got to do something!" she said. "There are bugs in my room!"

Sophia's room was across the hall from ours. I strode in, flipped on the light, and looked around.

"See 'em!" she shrieked. "All over the walls!"

"Sophia," I said. "There are no bugs on the walls. Go to sleep."

I turned, closed her door, and went back to bed.

I was deeply asleep when Sophia rapped on the bedroom door again, and we repeated the same scenario.

"Sophia," I said sternly, as if I were talking to a toddler, "do not wake me up again. There are absolutely no bugs on your walls. You need to get some sleep. Everything is fine."

I was asleep again when the third knock on the door came. "No," I shouted. "Go to bed. I'm asleep."

But she was going to wake up the rest of the household if I didn't come, so I went back to look for imaginary bugs. This time she had decided to help me out: Sophia had taken a tube of lipstick and had circled all the bug locations. The room's white walls were covered with dozens of bright red lipstick rings.

We had lots of adventures with Sophia. When she left us, she was sober and reconciled with her husband. We don't know the end of her story because we lost track of each other.

But we do know the end of the story for a young man named Rick, who entered our lives around the same time.

Glennis and I had started a coffeehouse for teenagers; we called it the Lighthouse and held it at the church every Friday evening. This was the early 1970s, and coffeehouses were big then. We would have a lot of music and singing with guitars, then a Bible study, some snacks and drinks. It was a great, low-key way for kids to gather together in a healthy atmosphere. Most Friday evenings we would have close to a hundred teenagers there.

One Saturday afternoon our daughter Kim was working at a church-sponsored car wash, trying to raise money for a trip. Kim was sixteen at the time, with a big smile, short blond hair, and bright blue eyes. Up drove a filthy, mud-caked car with a teenager named Rick Sendgraff at the wheel. Rick was rather taken with Kim, and while she washed his filthy car, he tried to ask her out on a date.

Kim said no, but as Rick continued to press her about it, she finally told him, "Okay, I'll go out with you, but we have to go to the place I choose."

"Okay," said Rick.

So the next Friday night, Rick came with Kim to the Lighthouse. I wasn't particularly thrilled when I saw him—he had long hair, ragged jeans, and didn't look as if he had a whole lot on the ball. Not the kind of guy I wanted my daughter to date. But as I talked with him, he seemed to be a decent kid, and later that night, when he brought Kim home, we gave him a Bible and talked with him about the Lord. In our living room, he prayed to receive Christ.

Rick became like part of our family, one of the dozens of kids who regularly dropped in and out of our house, sharing meals, playing Ping-Pong, and hanging out.

What we didn't know then, though, was that he was addicted to drugs and was supporting his habit by burglarizing homes right in our neighborhood.

Eventually Rick stopped coming around, and I lost track of him. We were so busy that I didn't think much about his absence—but later, Rick would play a key role in my life.

In 1972 Fairmont Foods moved its corporate headquarters from Omaha to Houston, and we were asked to move again. Glennis was open to it—she was a great sport—but we both felt that we had had enough of moving every few years. Our family was firmly entrenched in Omaha: our kids were in good schools, and we had strong relationships with so many close friends at our church. My schedule at Fairmont had continued to take its toll on our lives together, and I felt that this move to Houston represented a watershed, the opportunity to make a key decision regarding our future.

I was tired of travel. I was also ready for a change from corporate life. I've never been a person who relished office politics or the bureaucracy and constraints that are intrinsic elements of any corporation. I had toyed for years with the thought of owning my own company, and when Dick Kerns's family and ours vacationed together in Minnesota that summer, we brainstormed about starting our own snack-food manufacturing business. Dick had been in insurance for years; he would do sales. I would handle administration and production. I left Fairmont in August 1972, and we started KAP's—Kerns and Peterson—Foods.

We got financing through a bank in Omaha and got a line of credit for $100,000. When we were looking for a facility to house our company, we found a local plant that had been closed for about a year; it was equipped with the machinery we needed to get us cooking, so to speak. We had committed the whole project to God, and we believed that it was not mere coincidence that this plant in Omaha was for sale, with just the start-up equipment we needed, right then.

Although we started our manufacturing with just one product—potato chips—we soon were able to expand to other snacks such as cheese curls, popcorn, and caramel corn. Couch potatoes across Omaha and eventually throughout the Midwest started looking for the KAP's label. We were committed to top quality at an affordable price, but we weren't going to cut corners to make that happen.

We became profitable within a year or two, and the business went well. We didn't have the marketing dollars to create a strong brand image or to compete with the massive national companies, but we did develop a good business by selling private-label snacks to the local and regional grocery trade.

The business was great for two particular reasons. First,

I was home every night. At first Glennis and the kids didn't know what to do with me, but eventually we all got used to the new and radical routine of having Dad around during the week.

And second, the business integrated well with our household ministry. Some of the kids living with us ended up working at the plant, alongside our own children. Although the kids had to endure the 115-degree heat of the factory cooking area, they at least enjoyed the perks of standing at the conveyor belt and pulling off any potato chips that were too darkly cooked. I noticed that a lot of our products were getting eaten before they could even get bagged, but then there's absolutely nothing like a crisp, lightly salted potato chip, fresh and hot from the cooker.

So life went on. And then, one late spring day, a letter from Rick Sendgraff appeared in our mailbox. Its contents shocked me: Rick had been arrested, charged with burglary, convicted, and sent to prison. Behind bars, he had smuggled drugs into the institution and had been caught selling them to other inmates. He had been thrown into solitary confinement.

Rick had written his letter after several weeks in solitary. He was full of remorse, shame, and serious questions about his relationship with God. "Can I ever be forgiven?" he asked. "I turned away from God—can I still be saved?"

I wrote Rick back right away, assuring him of God's mercy and forgiveness. Then I wrote to the prison, asking permission to visit Rick. And three weeks later, I was on my way to the Nebraska State Penitentiary.

CHAPTER 5

Behind Bars

The Nebraska State Penitentiary is about fifty-five miles from Omaha. As I drove down I-80, I wasn't quite sure what I would encounter. I had never been to a prison before.

My first sight of the institution fit the pictures I had in my mind from old movies. The prison's high wire fences were ringed on top with spirals of jagged razor wire. I could see officers in the high guard towers, and it chilled me to think that they were armed, ready to fire if need be.

I parked my car and walked to the main entrance, my stomach churning as the huge, electronic gates clanged tight behind me. I felt claustrophobic already. I couldn't imagine what it would feel like to hear those gates slam shut and know that you could not get out for years, possibly a lifetime. It was eerie.

I cleared security, passing through a metal detector, and was escorted by officers into the visiting area, a large, ugly room filled with dozens of old, gouged wooden picnic tables. I looked around: I saw about seventy people in the room, male prisoners and their primarily female visitors.

Rick Sendgraff's name sounded over the PA system, and

ten minutes later Rick came in. We hugged, and he joined me at the picnic table. He was wearing prison blues and a white T-shirt. His hair was still long, and he had a dark mustache. We hadn't even seen one another for more than a year.

He seemed a little nervous, but that didn't last long. I told him about how Kim was doing and what was going on with our family. He told me about life in prison, particularly his time in solitary confinement. I shared some Scripture verses with Rick, paraphrasing verses like John 3:16 and Romans 10:9-10 as I talked, trying to assure Rick of the security of his relationship with God.

"Rick," I said, "you know that God forgives your sins. You know that God loved the world so much that he sent his only Son here so that whoever believes in him will live forever. You know that if you confess that Jesus is Lord and believe in your heart that God raised him from the dead, you'll be saved."

Rick looked at me, tears in his eyes. I could see that for him, like all of us, the idea of grace—that God loves us and saves us because of his choice, not because of our "worthiness"—was absolutely overwhelming. I could see his eyes light up with a new sense of hope. And as our visit went on, I saw that Rick Sendgraff—a convicted criminal locked up behind prison bars—now knew a greater sense of liberation than did many people who were walking around in the business world every day. He was *spiritually* free.

As we talked, an inmate who was getting ready to leave stopped at our table. His visitor had just left. "Dallen," Rick said, "I want you to meet my buddy. This is Mel Goebel."

Mel looked to be in his early twenties, with even white

teeth, long brown hair, and a big smile. He was into weight lifting, I could tell: his muscles were well defined, and he looked ruddily healthy, without the prison pallor of so many other inmates in the room. He was from Omaha; like Rick, Mel had decided to live for Christ in prison.

Mel told me his story. He had drifted through the first two years of his incarceration by smuggling marijuana into the prison. Then through another inmate, he realized that he wanted to live differently. The inmate told Mel that the only way he would break his addictions and heal his guilt was through a relationship with God. Mel confessed his sins and asked for God's forgiveness. He was flooded with a peace he had never known.

Becoming a Christian changed Mel's outlook on prison. Whereas he once had been consumed with thoughts about getting out, he said he now thought of prison as a monastery, a place where he could study the Bible, form close friendships, and practice his Christianity.

Hearing that, I shook my head. I had never been behind bars before, but certainly the thought of prison as a monastery had not been my first impression. *How incredible,* I thought. *Here, in the most hopeless of places, God gives people hope, joy, and purpose.*

Well, I was very impressed with Mel. And here was Rick, full of fresh hope. As we sat at that scarred old picnic table, we began to brainstorm about forming a real community of Christians in that prison. Why not start weekly Bible study meetings?

The next day, I wrote to the prison chaplain, explaining that I was a member of Calvary Lutheran Church in Omaha and that I wanted very much to start a Bible study in his prison. The chaplain, a fellow Lutheran, was all for it. So about three weeks later, I was back in prison, along with a good friend from church, Marv Kinman.

Every Friday evening, the prison showed movies to the inmates. As Marv and I entered the institution, the film was just beginning, and hundreds of inmates filled the narrow hallways, heading toward the auditorium. I didn't see any guards around. Most of the prisoners looked pretty tough, and all of them were much bigger than I. I just smiled at them and waved, my big Jerusalem Bible tucked under my slightly sweaty armpit.

We made it to the chapel alive. Rick, Mel, two other inmates, and Marv and I conducted our first in-prison Bible study. I didn't know what I was doing, but Marv's guitar was a great icebreaker. We sang Scripture songs and studied the Word. I also circulated a sign-in sheet for the inmates to fill out. I had put categories on it such as name, birthday, expected release date, and (much to my chagrin today) "offense." You just don't ask an inmate about his crime—but back then, I didn't know any better.

At any rate, by the end of that evening, I was absolutely exhilarated. The guys were so enthusiastic, so hungry to know more about God, so hungry for change in their lives. Marv and I both felt it was clear that God wanted us right back in that prison every Friday night.

So that's what we did. The next week there were seven guys, the week after that about fifteen, and six months later we had seventy-five men coming every week—out of an institution of three hundred thirty inmates. Once a prisoner had come to the study three times, we would present him with a Bible with his name engraved in gold on the cover.

The study's growth rate had little to do with Marv and me. It came from the Christian character of Rick, Mel, and the others. The inmates in that institution could see that Christ really could change a person's life and give him real, muscular hope.

In prison, just as on the outside, you can't make generalizations about people. Some of the inmates I met were highly intelligent. Others were functionally handicapped. Some were remorseful about their crimes and the lifestyle that had brought them into prison, and they wanted desperately to change their lives. Others were belligerent and cultivated their defiance.

But most of them did have one thing in common: they had known a tremendous amount of pain in their lives. They had known physical, sexual, and emotional abuse. They had been rejected, scorned, and betrayed. They felt hopeless.

Of course those violations are no excuse for committing crimes. But as my friends and I sought to bring to these men the hope and new life that comes with repentance, we had to enter into their pain.

As I listened to them, cared for them, and became their friend, I realized how different my life had been from theirs. I had had such an easy life. I hadn't known deep trauma or adversities. No matter how open I was, I could not fully empathize with their misery.

But I could point them to One who could.

That's what Christianity is all about. Instead of sitting in heaven, watching our misery from afar, God came to earth in the form of a person. In Jesus Christ, God himself became a man—and experienced the vulnerability and pain of what it means to be a human being.

Incredible!

I found that in prison, when men truly understood the lengths to which God himself had gone to enter into their pain—and then provide the full payment for their sins—they were absolutely overwhelmed. Some of them, like some people on the outside, had hard hearts that they just would not open to love, even divine love.

But many inmates listened to the gospel, and their hearts broke open. They received the love of God. And their lives were changed forever.

My own faith deepened dramatically as a result, and I gained far more than I gave to those men in the penitentiary. When you see a condemned killer change from a mean, tough, vile person to a soft-spoken, loving human being, you know you've seen a miracle!

Meanwhile, outside the barbed wire, the prison ministry was also bringing fresh vitality to our church.

First, Glennis signed on. Within a week of my first visit to the institution, Glennis had gotten on Mel's visiting list, so she could go with me. On Sundays we would pack a picnic lunch, drive to Lincoln, and eat in the prison yard with Rick and Mel. I've always marveled at my wife: Here she was, with five children and usually a few others living with us as well—a very busy schedule—but when I proposed that we start dining in prison every Sunday, she didn't bat an eye. She says it's because she comes from hardy German stock, and that's what has given her the strength to put up with my crazy ideas over the last forty years. I think it's because she is a compassionate woman who helps others whenever she can.

At any rate, there were eventually about twenty-five church couples who followed Glennis's lead, got onto various prisoners' visiting lists, and began meeting with and mentoring these young men.

That Christmas, I wanted to do something special for the men in the Bible study. I announced to our church congregation that we would be giving gifts to the Christian inmates, and anyone who wanted to pitch in could buy an appropriate present, wrap it, and get it to me and the other prison volunteers.

The congregation responded enthusiastically, and by the week before Christmas, we had dozens of brightly wrapped presents—large, medium, small, red, green, gold—wedged into my Ford station wagon. Even though I'd been going into the prison for months, I was still pretty naive. I had no idea that there was no way the prison officials would allow wrapped gifts to enter the institution; for all they knew, all those lovely ribboned boxes were full of drugs, files, firearms, hacksaws, explosive devices, you name it.

No, I just drove my gift-laden station wagon up to the prison gates and explained to the guard that I had presents for the inmates in my Bible study. He knew me by now, of course, but he shook his head back and forth and said he would have to check with the warden.

I sat in my car for a few minutes, the thought beginning to dawn on me that we might have to unwrap every present and pass each one through security and that I might not get to the Bible study group for a very, very long time. And then I saw the

gate officer again, smiling and nodding at me. The next thing
I knew, the huge prison gates were rolling open, and the officer
was motioning my car—not toward the usual parking lot, but
right up to the front steps of the prison itself!

Unbelievable. And then, to top it off, the officers let Mel,
Rick, and several of the other inmates out to help us unload
the car and carry all those gifts into the prison chapel. I suppose our innocent enthusiasm—and a little bit of Christmas
good will—overrode the usual prison precautions. It was a
tremendous encouragement for the guys in the Bible study.

But that little Christmas miracle happened only once.
The next year, when I asked about doing the same thing, I
was flatly turned down. We continued providing gifts—but
through normal channels.

In April of 1976, I went to the mayor's prayer breakfast in
Omaha. It was a yearly event that I usually attended, but I was
particularly curious to go that year because Chuck Colson was
the main speaker. I, like just about everyone else in America,
had followed the Watergate scandal and the demise of President Nixon's administration. I had followed Chuck Colson's
notorious career and his widely publicized Christian conversion. I was eager to hear him speak.

The crowd that morning, about fifteen hundred Omahans,
included many who were, to say the least, quite skeptical about
Colson's alleged conversion. But as I listened to Chuck speak—
with his characteristic intellectual insight and spiritual passion—I realized that this was a man who had been deeply broken and humbled, and as a result he was deeply committed to
helping people in prison.

Although we were very different personalities with very

different experiences, I identified with Chuck's sense of mission. He, like the guys in the prison Bible study, was my brother in Christ. (In fact, we had both gone into prison for the very first time the same week in 1974—except that Chuck had gone in as an inmate and I as a volunteer.)

At that point I had no idea of the key role he would play in my life, both personally and in terms of my business.

Later that year, both Mel Goebel and Rick Sendgraff were released from prison.

Release, though sweet, can be a dangerous time for many inmates. Even for those who come to know Christ in prison, adjusting to life on the outside is a very difficult transition. Prison is a highly structured environment, where most choices—when to eat, sleep, work, where to go, what to do—are made for you. Presented with the countless options of life on the outside, many inmates falter and stumble. Many lack the skills to find a good job; all face the stigma of being an ex-convict. Many have fragmented families and few friends—except for their old friends from life on the streets. Faced with such pressures and obstacles, many ex-prisoners, in spite of their best intentions, fail and fall on the outside. Many end up right back behind bars.

We didn't want that to happen to Rick, Mel, and the other young men coming out of the prison in Lincoln. Rick did construction work; Mel came back home to Omaha and started working with me at KAP's Foods as a truck driver. He, Rick, and a number of the other former inmates joined our church, Calvary Lutheran. We probably had six or seven former inmates living in various homes in the congregation. It was a wonderful ministry for the ex-prisoners, many of whom were minorities. And their presence gave tremendous vitality to our insular, all-white congregation, because through them we had the opportunity to learn to be the kind of community a biblical church is supposed to be.

There were a few exceptions, of course. I remember one Sunday one of the older members of the church caught up with me ouside the sanctuary, poking his finger into my chest. "How many more of these convicts are you going to bring to Calvary?" he said with a scowl.

I don't know if he ever caught the exquisite irony of his words.

One of my golfing partners was Ed Danitschek, pastor of another local Lutheran church. Ed's daughter, Jane, was our congregation's administrator and organist. During golf outings with Ed, I would talk about Mel and how well he was doing. Mel went back to school, got his GED, and enrolled in college. He was growing in Christ, doing well, and Ed was excited for him.

Then Mel and Jane's friendship began to grow. They started dating. Ed wasn't quite as enthusiastic about his daughter's dating an ex-con, but gradually that changed, which was good because Mel and Jane were married in 1979. Rick and I were both ushers in their wedding.

For Rick's part, he went into sales and sold cash registers in Omaha. Later he moved to Dallas, got married, and started his own cash-register company. Glennis and I would see him every once in a while over the years; he was doing well and honored me immensely when he named his youngest son Dallen.

As I look back, it's amazing to see how our lives were inter-

twined, from that first day so long ago when Rick showed up
at Kim's car wash, through his bringing me into prison, to the
Bible study, to the ongoing prison ministry that has been so
important to me ever since. I loved him like a son.

One Friday night in June 1997, Rick was in Dallas, driving
home to his wife and children. Someone tried to steal his car
and rob him—we don't know quite what happened. But in the
robbery attempt, Rick was shot and killed.

I will never get over the shock of Rick's death. But I take
comfort when I think back to that prison visit in 1974, when
Rick and I sat before an open Bible at that old, rugged picnic
table. I think of those Bible verses I shared with him that day,
remembering so clearly what I said: "Rick, you know that God
forgives your sins. You know that God loved the world so
much that he sent his only Son here—so that *whoever believes
in him will live forever.*"

And when I think of that, although the tears still come
to my eyes, I know I will see Rick Sendgraff again one day.

We kept visiting the prison in Lincoln for twelve years.
I loved the inmates; it was so exciting to see them change and
grow as the unique hope that only Christ can give began to
take root in their lives.

And, as with any kind of ministry, I received far more
than I gave. I might have been teaching the Friday night Bible
study, but I was learning far more than the inmates as I tried
to equip them with faith, love, and hope, even in the midst
of tough circumstances.

All of that growth was good because I was about to
encounter my own challenges, with the impending failure of
KAP's Foods.

CHAPTER 6

When the Chips Were Down

During the end of 1978 and through the summer of 1979, commodity costs began to soar. And as potato and oil prices continued to go up, up, up, my eyes were firmly focused right on the bottom line at KAP's Foods. As a small company, we weren't able to absorb the higher costs of doing business, and back in those days, consumers were sensitive about snack-food prices. Grocers and manufacturers alike were convinced that people wouldn't pay more than $.69 for a bag of potato chips.

So, as commodity prices ballooned, margins that were already thin narrowed even more. Then a competitor from Des Moines decided to enter the Omaha private-label snack market; he cut prices even lower. As I've mentioned, we were committed to producing the best possible products, and as those potato, oil, and packaging costs kept escalating, we still refused to compromise quality for price. So we could not slash our prices.

My partner, Dick Kerns, and I talked and prayed about our snack crisis; we did everything we could, but we were careening closer and closer to bankruptcy. Then, incredibly enough, we were able to sell KAP's, just in time.

I came home from that sales closing and began to take stock. I was forty-two years old. I had been in corporate life for thirteen years with Fairmont. I had loved it, but I didn't want to go back into a large corporation. Then I'd invested seven years in KAP's. That experience had taught me that I never again wanted to be a small fish in a big sea controlled by competitors. I wanted to do something big.

As headhunters called me and various companies pursued me for executive positions, I interviewed for several rather promising corporate slots. I was offered some very good jobs, with nice salaries, plenty of perks. But they just didn't strike a chord with me. I usually go by my gut in life's big decisions, and my gut was clearly not excited about a return to corporate life.

We spent that summer at our lake home in Minnesota, just down the big hill from the farmhouse where I was born. Glennis and I walked the country roads there and prayed, "Lord, what next?"

We took comfort in Proverbs 3:5-6: "Trust in the Lord with all your heart and lean not on your own understanding; in all your ways acknowledge him, and he will make your paths straight."

We just didn't know what path God would put us on.

I did know that I wanted to be on my own in the new business. Dick Kerns and I are close friends to this day, and our partnership at KAP's had been great. But invariably, in a partnership you each have your own expectations, and they are never the same. And there can be different levels of commitment as well, making it hard to work things out. So I was determined to go it alone, or, I should say, go it with Glennis.

We were already partners for life—why not take our team into the business world?

I also knew, based on my earlier experience, that I didn't want to be in a business where I'd get caught in the middle again, helplessly crunched between suppliers' costs and customers' demands. To me the service arena seemed to be the cutting-edge opportunity of the future. It had no high inventories, high receivables, or high payables.

Once I did a little research, I found that 48 percent of all women were employed outside the home, and that rate was growing by one percent a year. (Today that figure is over 60 percent, and at 75 percent for all women between the ages of thirty and fifty.)

I hadn't really focused before on how powerful this trend was because it hadn't touched my life: Glennis had never worked outside the home. But I realized that the typical American family was quite different from my own.

Increasingly, husbands and wives were *both* at the office all day. Yet studies were showing that it was still *women* who performed the bulk of the housecleaning work. I knew from my mother's strict training when I was growing up just how hard housecleaning really was, and I realized that already-harried working women would probably do just about anything to get the cleaning burden off their backs.

Right around that same time, a friend from church had started cleaning houses as a way to bring in extra income. She had been flooded with calls and ended up with so much business that she asked Glennis and a few other friends to pitch in and give her a hand.

Glennis jumped right in to help, and as I saw the demand

for housecleaning right in our own backyard in Omaha, I realized that the statistical trends and the conclusions I was drawing from my demographic research were right on target.

I also discovered that while there were many small local cleaning companies, both in Omaha and across the country, there was no nationwide maid service in the U.S. at that time.

Hmm.

I considered other options. I thought about a handyman service, or a carpet-cleaning business, or drapes-and-window cleaning. But even as I toyed with these, my gut was getting excited about starting a maid-service business.

By October, I was drawing up a business plan. I wanted to develop a prototype maid service in Omaha for a year, and then, for some strange reason, I knew I wanted to franchise.

I didn't know the first thing about it, and I didn't even talk to anyone in the franchise industry. That probably wasn't wise, but, on the other hand, at least I had no preconceived notions about franchising. In my gut I had a feeling that if I could build the right business, I could sell it over and over and over.

In my years with Fairmont, I had traveled throughout America, and I just knew that if there was such a need for housecleaning right in Omaha, then how much more so in other parts of the country. I knew that if I could make it work in Omaha, it would play in Peoria—and, I hoped, everywhere else.

The first issue, though, was to come up with a good, strong name for the business. I carried a yellow legal pad with me and would jot down names whenever they came to mind. Even our children pitched in with suggestions. We would sit in the living room late at night shouting things at each other like

"Helping Hands!" "Home Helpers!" "Willing Workers!" "Paradise People!" "Feather Dusters!" "Snappy Homemakers!" "Spiffy Dusters!"

Eventually we would all just give up and go to bed.

"Swift Sweepers!" Kim shouted one day.

"No," said Glennis. "Too hard to say."

"Weary-Free Homemakers!" someone said.

"Huh?" the rest of us responded.

"Quality Home Cleaners!" said someone else.

"Too plain," I said. "We need something zippy and positive."

"How about Speed Queens?" someone suggested.

"Sounds like drag-car racing."

"Crown Cleaners?"

"Sounds like the dentist."

"Leisure Ladies?"

"Sounds as if we should call in the vice squad."

All this went on for weeks. One day while I was driving, something from a billboard caught my eye, and I jotted the name "Merry Maids" on my yellow pad. It was number twelve on a list of thirty-five names.

To keep us all from going crazy, I enlisted the help of Tom Guy, with whom I had worked at Fairmont Foods. Since then he had helped Godfather's pizza build their national reputation. Godfather's was, in fact, the only franchise I had ever really noticed. It had started in Omaha in the mid-1970s and was on its way to great success.

I couldn't afford Tom's official services, but he met with me one Saturday morning. We drank coffee, ate donuts, and brainstormed about my new business's image and plan. I appreciated Tom's tremendous energy and creativity. He

worked through my list of names, and together we settled on
Merry Maids. Tom felt it was the most memorable, had a good
ring to it, and could be marketed well—and I trusted his
instincts!

After meeting with Tom, I hired an attorney to move forward with our articles of incorporation and registration. He
felt the Merry Maids name was so strong that I should not
begin to use it until it was copyright protected.

That done, I contracted with a design firm Tom recom-
mended and on Christmas Eve presented my family with six
different logo options. We were at my parents' farmhouse in
Minnesota, watching the snow swirl past the kitchen windows,
having consumed our usual Yuletide feast—lutefisk, roast beef,
lefse, mashed potatoes, glorified rice, and all the trimmings.
After dinner, I enthusiastically spread the logos out on the
kitchen table, excited about getting Merry Maids off the
ground.

My mother looked over the logos, smiling politely, and
then she sighed. "Oh, Dallen," she said. "You've always been so
successful. I just can't understand why you would want to go
into the housecleaning business!"

Most of my family and friends weren't quite as candid as
my mother, but they were thinking the same thing. Maid service just didn't have the prestigious image of professions like
banking or the law. Everyone thought that the upward mobil-
ity I had enjoyed throughout my professional life had taken
an abrupt U-turn and that I was single-mindedly careening in
exactly the wrong direction.

But I didn't let other people's opinions deter my enthusiasm. I had done the research, and I knew there was a hole in

the market. I knew that this business was aimed right at the heart of two very powerful forces: the increasing numbers of women in the workplace, and the intrinsic need for a woman's home to be a haven after a hard day at that workplace.

Late on Christmas Day we drove back to Omaha, and on December 26, 1979, we ran our very first advertisement, several succinct lines in the classified section of the *Omaha World Herald:* "Professional housecleaning, call 345-5599."

Then came the first phone call, the realtor's seemingly innocent request to clean an elderly woman's small home—that infamous job that resulted in sixty-six backbreaking hours of work for me and my bedraggled family, all for sixty-six rather overearned dollars.

But it was a beginning.

CHAPTER 7

From Rags to More Rags

We continued to run the two-line ad in the Omaha newspaper, and calls continued to come in. Not a lot at first, but they were steady. Glennis and the kids cleaned; I pitched in when needed but focused mostly on developing the business. I also made sure that I went out to inspect the homes before I gave any estimates. Our $66 disaster taught me that lesson right away.

In our first month of business, we grossed $800. Around the same time, we hired our first part-time employees—friends who were excited about our new venture and wanted to pick up a little extra cash. (Our daughter Karma was actually our first paid employee, starting at the royal sum of $5 an hour. A University of Nebraska student, she ended up paying for her entire college education—with the exception of her first and last semesters—through her work for Merry Maids.)

In fact, I can't say enough about how all our kids helped. Just as Glennis's and my parents had instilled a hearty work ethic in us, we had tried to pass that on to our children. They had all cleaned from the time they were tiny; they were quite familiar with my obsession for spotless walls and streak-free windows. They grumbled good-naturedly—they couldn't believe that my cleaning fixation had actually turned into a business—but they all jumped right in and worked to exhaustion to help get Merry Maids up and running.

Glennis designed the maids' first uniforms and whipped them up on her sewing machine: yellow aprons with green accents that the maids wore with khaki pants and white shirts. We bought more vacuum cleaners and made up fresh cleaning kits every night. I had learned about mixing chemicals while I was at Fairmont Foods. Late at night, like mad scientists, Glennis and I would go down to the basement to compose our cleaning concoctions in gallon-size pickle jars.

As we experimented with our Merry Maids cleaning solutions, I drew from family memories. I remembered from my childhood how a clean house *smelled* clean, so I experimented with different disinfectant fragrances. Lemon was popular in the cleaning market back then—this was in 1980—but I remembered the cozy smell of my mother's hot cinnamon rolls, fresh from the oven, and I came up with a cinnamon-scented deodorizer that is a Merry Maids hallmark to this day.

Every morning the maids would gather in our living room. We would drink coffee, laugh, and, if business was good, eat honey-glazed donuts. I would hand out the cleaning assignments for the day, and then everyone would troop on out for a hard day's work. There was a tremendous sense of camaraderie. We were working hard, but we were having fun.

Two months after starting the business, on March 12, 1980, Glennis and I celebrated our twenty-fifth wedding anniversary. Our daughter Kim and her husband, Pete, visited from Minneapolis for the occasion. They could sense our growing

excitement about Merry Maids. Although business was modest, we were more than doubling our number of customers
every month, and Glennis and I were no longer able to handle
everything on our own. Glennis was training and supervising
our maids, and I was handling all the administrative, sales,
and operations aspects of our fledgling company. And already
we were getting our first inquiries about franchising, so I was
developing the prototype of our franchise systems.

Kim and Pete decided they wanted to jump right in. In
typical family style, they acted quickly: they bought a house
in Omaha that very weekend.

They both learned the business from the ground up. Pete
did everything from bidding jobs to maintaining equipment,
scheduling maids, and cleaning houses if need be.

I cleaned too, of course—but only for customers who
weren't home. I didn't want our clients to realize that we were
so tight staffed that the president of the company was the one
cleaning their houses!

One day our daughter Kris, who was pregnant at the time,
was helping me clean a house. Then the customer came home
unexpectedly. I greeted the woman at the door, smiling widely.

"Well, hello!" I said. "The other maid working with Kris
should be here any minute."

The woman left, and then Kris and I raced through the
house, cleaning madly.

Another time Kris and I cleaned the home of a young
businessman. Afterward he left us a note, complaining that
the tops of the mirrors had not been dusted. Kris looked at
me with her eyebrows down. She knew that I had cleaned the
mirrors.

"Dad!" she said sternly. "I know you're short. But you've got to figure out a way to reach the tops of those mirrors!"

One day after I had graduated from—or perhaps been fired from—cleaning houses myself, a couple called me about a job. I went to their home to do the estimate, and it looked fairly reasonable. The husband and wife were both doctors, worked long hours, and had two large, longhaired dogs. I could understand why they needed maid service.

A week later Glennis arrived at their home early one morning, ready to clean. I'll never forget her phone call.

"Dallen!" she sputtered. "I don't know what it was like when you saw this place, but I can tell you right now that they have not let these dogs out for a very long time, and this house is covered with dog poop! You get yourself over here now! This is not what I'm here for!"

I sped to the doctors' home, got my wife out of there, and dealt with the couple. They were very upset that we declined to clean up after their dogs. But poop removal has just never been one of Merry Maids' listed services.

Another time Glennis arrived at the home of a Jewish woman who had talked with me about a basic cleaning, but when Glennis got there the woman explained that she wanted to prepare for Passover. She walked Glennis through the home, pointing out all of the cabinets she wanted cleaned out, their contents dusted and reconfigured. Glennis looked over dozens of cupboards filled with hundreds of spice jars, old shoe boxes, knickknacks, and junk, and her eyes glazed over.

I gave Glennis a break after that. She was at home on phone duty one day, and a woman called to complain that the Merry Maids hadn't done a good job on her home.

Glennis knew that our daughters Karma and Kim had cleaned that particular house. She told the customer she'd call her back and then asked the girls about it. She believed them when they told her they had done their usual fine job.

Then the customer called back, still in a fury that her house was not cleaned properly. Glennis, never a diplomat, told her in no uncertain terms that she knew that the maids who had cleaned that house were above reproach and that if the woman had problems with the cleaning, they were in her own head.

Then she hung up on the customer.

The woman called back immediately, and Glennis, furious, just let the phone ring and ring.

When I got back home, Glennis was still simmering.

"Whatever happened to 'the customer is always right'?" I asked mildly.

"Not when they mess with my daughters," Glennis muttered.

I called the client back. "I'm so sorry," I apologized. "I'll just have to have a word with our office staff about phone protocol."

But as we look back, Glennis and I agree that in spite of the headaches, those early days of the business were fun.

We were also rather purposeful about our intentions with our new company. Whatever its outcomes, we were determined to work hard, as the Bible says, as if we were working for the Lord. Our faith in him also served as the foundation for our four corporate objectives. These were life goals I had embraced for a long time in terms of my commitment to God and my desire to help people reach their potential. Now they became our corporate principles as well and are part of the Merry Maids ethos to this day. They are to

- honor God in all we do,
- help people develop,
- pursue excellence, and
- grow profitably.

I believed that if we pursued these principles, we would enjoy real success. As I'll relate more in the second half of this book, success did not mean just the financial rewards of a profitable bottom line, but the *real success* that comes from serving God and our fellow human beings to the best of our opportunity and ability. I knew if I set my sights on that real success, the money would follow.

But back in those early days, while it was clear that we were pursuing the first three objectives, we weren't yet sure that we were going to ever make it on the profitability front!

In an effort to grow, we kicked off our first advertising campaign. Our door-to-door experience taught us some pretty basic lessons.

I had one hundred simple ad flyers printed, and one morning Mel Goebel, my son Brett, and I went to a local condominium complex to distribute them. We carefully stuck one in each resident's door. When we got home about three hours later, Glennis was waiting.

"The condo manager called," she said. "You've got to go back and get those flyers out of there."

We went back gloomily to undo our morning's work, but we were heartened to discover that about half of the ads had already been picked up by the residents. In the next few days, we saw our calls go up significantly.

That experience told me that flyers could work, but I also realized that we had targeted wrong. Even though condo dwellers were mostly two-income couples, they weren't as likely to hire out for maid service as owners of single family homes were. I realized that our primary market was—and is to this day—upper middle-class homes.

We began to target such homes in West Omaha and developed what has probably been Merry Maids' most successful yet most humble marketing tool over the years.

Federal regulations prohibited us from stuffing mailboxes with advertising flyers. We could leave flyers in a homeowner's front door, of course, but they could easily blow away. Then we thought about those Do Not Disturb signs in hotels. Using our signature colors, bright yellow and clean green, we designed doorhangers that could be put on residential doorknobs. The front said, "Hang on to this," and the back gave a list of reasons why Merry Maids was worth hanging on to, along with our phone number.

Later, doorhangers would become key to any franchise owner's success. Research showed that if an owner would select a high-potential neighborhood of 250 homes and distribute doorhangers on Tuesdays, Wednesdays, and Thursdays for four consecutive weeks, his or her return would typically look like this: a .5 percent response in week one, 1 percent in week two, 2 percent in week three, and 2 to 3 percent in week four.

Although doorhangers weren't particularly exciting, they worked. I always thought of our plan to distribute them as something like a Weight Watchers' diet plan. You had to stick with it, slow and steady, in order to get results. Over the years, some franchise owners would use doorhangers for a week and then give up and try something else. They wanted instant gratification. But in business gains, just as in weight loss, it just doesn't work that way. Even today, Merry Maids' largest franchise, which does more than $2 million in annual sales, continues to put out hundreds of simple doorhangers every week.

My initial plan had been to develop the business in Omaha for one year and then to move into franchising. But things started moving faster than I had anticipated.

Our neighbors, who had long been quite gracious, began to complain about the parking problems outside our home. Team members' cars lined the curbs, and the workers bustled in and out of our house, carrying vacuums, buckets, and other cleaning supplies. We were disrupting the peace and quiet of the neighborhood.

So on June 1, 1980, we moved into our first rental space, a three-office area with a small supply room. Its advantage was that it was on one of the main thoroughfares in Omaha. We put up a big Merry Maids sign—Professional Homecleaning— and every career woman driving to downtown Omaha in the morning, and on her weary way back home in the evening, saw that sign beckoning. Not a few of them called us!

Around the same time, we added our very first Merry Maids franchise. Ever since Pete had joined us, I had been freed to concentrate on developing our operations manual and our franchising agreements. So our practices were set out on paper as cleanly as I could articulate them. Now we would see if they could be replicated!

Our old friends Norm and Marge Jorgensen were game to develop the first Merry Maids spin-off from our first company-owned franchise. Theirs would be Franchise #101. (I started the numbering at 100 to create a feeling of momentum. It would feel rather lonely to be Franchise #1!) The Jorgensens were wonderful people in Fremont, Nebraska, hardworking farmers who had fallen on hard times. We gave them the franchise for free, and they ended up doing very well with it.

I gave away the next four franchises as well. One went to my brother Jim in Willmar, Minnesota. Another went to our printer's wife in Omaha—I bartered Merry Maids franchise supplies for printing jobs. Another went to Gene McNamara, an old buddy from Fairmont days.

We also gave a franchise to one of our first employees, Carol. She had helped us out as a maid, and when her husband, Richard, was released from prison, the family needed a fresh start. So we gave a franchise to Carol and Rich, and it worked out beautifully. Rich later became our training director, taking the elements of his own franchise success and passing those principles on in the training of hundreds of other new franchise owners.

So as you might expect, the early days of Merry Maids had a strong friends-and-family feel. By September our older son, Brian, and his wife, Kim, moved from Minnesota to Omaha to help us as well. They both pitched right in, doing everything from cleaning to washing rags to setting up our first resource center. Every facet of our new business was in the development stage. Their help was invaluable as we continued to get our systems up and running.

And Kim served as my first full-time administrative

assistant. I had no idea how proficient she was until she unexpectedly left when their first child arrived a month early, and I was left high and dry without her expertise, trying to finish our first operations manual on my own!

Our family's support and enthusiasm was tremendous—and certainly from the very beginnings of my maid-service idea, I had known I could use our network of relatives and friends to develop a large, successful housecleaning business in Omaha. That would be relatively easy.

But I wanted more. I knew that others could take our ideas and run with them. And I knew from my own personality that there would be immense satisfaction—not to mention financial gain—in watching that happen.

As we helped our fledgling Merry Maids offices take off in the closing months of 1980, I felt an exhilarating sense of momentum and potential. I also felt a sense of confirmation: God had led us in the right direction. The business that Glennis and I had begun to establish—through the time-tested triad of sweat, tears, and toil—*could* be replicated. As we were beginning to taste success, we could pass it on to others.

Thus affirmed, I continued to believe that our business potential was huge.

First, I knew that if our franchises in Nebraska could make it, then Merry Maids could make it everywhere across the United States. My demographic studies regarding the market situation had been right on target: there was a definite felt need for housecleaning, and there was enough disposable income out there to pay for it.

So, second, the opportunity was absolutely ripe for the picking to the company that could provide dependable, excellent service. That meant that entrepreneurs who took on a Merry Maids franchise would enjoy the fruits of success. Not right away, of course. But through hard work, perseverance, and adherence to the Merry Maids model, people really could improve their own financial situation. And then they could pass on their success in the lives of their children.

Helping people develop in such a way had always been at the heart of my vision. Beginning to see that vision realized, even in small ways, gave me a thrilling sense of energy for the future.

CHAPTER 8

Good Clean Fun

As the oldest of nine children, my twin brother, Dale, and I did our share of housecleaning, both inside and out. And as we learned very early on from our mother—who had very exacting standards—cleaning a home properly is a tough job. From the beginning of Merry Maids' history, I wished I could have gone on national television and described to men everywhere how hard it is to maintain a clean home. Many men do not carry their share of the workload in a household, and I suspected that if they did housecleaning once in a while, they would realize that their household needed some help. I imagined that our customer calls would go through the roof.

One of our first business concerns was to systematize our cleaning practices. In the beginning we established clear procedures called "cleaning for show." My thought was that elements of cleaning are done primarily for two senses—sight and smell—and when those work together, they convince customers of the quality of our cleaning operation.

We standardized and refined our cleaning practices in several key ways.

First, Merry Maids work in teams. We divided the team's cleaning tasks between wet work and dry work. Both tasks begin at the top or back of the home and work forward until the team literally cleans its way out the front door.

I did time studies with teams of two, three, four, and five, and it became clear to me that teams of two were the most efficient. But whether we were working with two or with three, the team needed a designated person to be in charge. So we devised a system of captains and mates. The more experienced captain would direct the work, following the instructions printed out for that particular home.

These instructions came from our data management system. Based on my walk-through and estimate with the homeowner, we would highlight specific areas of concern. This specialized attention became one of our greatest strengths. It let customers know that we were listening, that we cared about what they cared about. It also built a tremendous sense of customer loyalty. Cleaning is one thing. Tailoring the cleaning to meet a person's taste is another, and it made our early customers realize that we offered something better than the competition. We tried to entertain our clients' quirks—within reason—like the customer who wanted the little pillows on her poodle's bed plumped and placed just so.

The teams would clean each room from the top down, in a clockwise direction, from vacuuming the ceilings to vacuuming and grooming the carpet or scrubbing the floors on hands and knees.

We tested ten different vacuums before selecting a model that was very light, was easy to maintain, and had beater bars that not only vacuumed but also raised the nap on a carpet, enhancing its look. We literally groomed the carpets.

We color coded all of our self-developed cleaning products as well as the cleaning cloths. That way, a worker in a hurry could simply grab the right bottle and the right cleaning cloth without needing to stop to read the label on the solution bottle.

In those early days—and today—we dealt with a lot of customer eccentricities. In fact, we welcomed most of them. They kept life interesting for the team members. One customer would sprinkle spare change throughout her home, in hard-to-vacuum corners, underneath sofa cushions, on high shelves. Our teams delighted in thoroughly cleaning and finding all these little treasures, then piling up the change on the customer's kitchen table to find when she got home from work.

Another client surprised one of our teams by being at home when they arrived, greeting them at the front door draped in a bath towel. He was a one-time customer.

For these and other adventures, our maids were insured and bonded, and Merry Maids handled all social security, taxes, and workers' compensation matters. (Far too many people who hire mom-and-pop independent cleaning services— which do tend to be slightly cheaper than companies like Merry Maids—fail to understand the serious consequences of violating federal and state laws on those fronts.)

Along with standardizing our cleaning and business practices, I had to figure out a way to accurately estimate and bid cleaning services for potential customers. We needed a system that could be easily transferred to franchise owners while remaining as nationally consistent as possible.

I did a variety of time studies with cleaning teams and

then segmented each hour of work. I tried segments of five, ten, and fifteen minutes; quarter-hour segments seemed the most practical.

For an estimate, I would go through a house room by room and look at how much clutter there was to pick up. I would determine how long the actual cleaning would take and then calculate it into quarter-hour segments.

Various factors determined how long a specific job would take. A carpeted bathroom, for example, would always be cleaned faster than a tiled one because tile had to be cleaned on hands and knees. A room with lots of mirrors would take a chunk of time. In the living room or family room, glass-topped coffee tables were more time-consuming to clean than wooden ones. A cluttered kitchen filled with appliances was of course more of a time eater than a streamlined kitchen. Wood floors would have to be vacuumed and then cleaned on hands and knees. Kids' rooms whose floors were covered with piles of toys would always take a while; the cleaners would have to get down to the carpet level—sort of like an archeological dig—in order to vacuum.

Of course, no two homes are the same. But the quarter system was my best bet for standardizing estimates. Once I'd calculated the number of quarters, then I'd plug the rate factor in. This would vary depending on local demographics. I was dreaming big, even then, and I knew that an Omaha rate would vary greatly from the cost of living in Los Angeles or Washington, D.C., or Boston.

Why not? I thought.

After giving away the first five franchises, things began to roll along. In February 1981 Glennis and I took our usual ski trip to Colorado and spent time with our former pastor and his wife, Bob and Carolyn Ellison. Typically, they were very encouraging as they listened to our excitement about Merry Maids. Bob set us up with Bill McCarthy, a friend who had been trying to get a local housecleaning business off the ground.

When I met with Bill and his wife, Sue, on a Sunday evening, they were interested yet skeptical of the notion of a franchise company. They bought a franchise, however, for $4,500. Today they are still with Merry Maids and have the distinction of being the longest-term franchise owners. That initial franchise they bought is worth hundreds of thousands of dollars today!

In 1981 we sold twenty-three franchises and were expanding across the center of the country, from Minneapolis to Denver, Dallas, and Houston. By mid-1982 we had fifty franchises. More than two-thirds of them had come from referrals of existing owners, so there was a strong sense of company excitement and momentum that bubbled up from the owners themselves.

The balance of our prospective owners heard about Merry Maids through our advertising in the business-opportunities sections of various Sunday newspapers. (I found that it would take three consecutive Sunday ads in any given city newspaper before the response rate would pick up.) Franchise owners then, as now, came from a variety of backgrounds in small business, corporate life, insurance, or education. But all were looking to run their own small business and saw Merry Maids' growing success as a good train to climb aboard.

One of my greatest pleasures was getting to know our new franchise owners when they came to Omaha for their week of Merry Maids training. We'd take them through our procedures from top to bottom. They cleaned houses themselves, so they could appreciate the hard work they would be hiring others to do. They learned our systems, products, and policies.

But most important, they learned about us. By this I mean they got to know our home-office staff as individuals; we spent as much time with them as we could, both in and outside the office. During the laughter—and sometimes the tears—of those training weeks, we forged friendships that have lasted for decades.

The week always culminated with a formal dinner in our home. Glennis and I used our best china, glowing candles, fragrant flowers, and typically served juicy Omaha steaks.

We did everything we could to make those evenings special. I believe that intimate atmosphere in our home helped to create Merry Maids' strong sense of family connection, particularly as those franchise owners left us and went back to their homes to make their new businesses succeed.

So our early franchise growth was exciting. But in the spring of 1982 I faced a serious practical problem. The life of any small business depends on cash flow, and I didn't have any. Actually, I had plenty of flow but very little cash. We had never borrowed money for the business, and I didn't want to start now.

A young woman named Cheryl Anderson had bought one of our franchises. When Cheryl came to our home office in Omaha for training, she stayed with her parents, who lived in the area. During her training week, Cheryl got even more excited about the Merry Maids concept. She told me one morning that she had talked with her father at some length about Merry Maids as a business opportunity.

"My dad says he'll call you tomorrow," she told me.

When I got home that evening, I told Glennis, "We really need to pray that this guy will be open to buying a franchise, because we won't even have the money to make payroll next time if something doesn't happen."

"Well," said Glennis, ever practical, "God knows our needs."

The next day Cheryl's father called, and when I arrived at his office, it was clear that I didn't even need to sell Merry Maids to him; Cheryl had already done that for me. Within five minutes her father bought three franchises, at $9500 each. That $28,500 got us over the hump, and over the years that followed, Merry Maids didn't face another cash-flow crisis.

During the course of the business I had, of course, talked a lot about it with my brother Dale. I had appreciated his insights and ideas; it seemed only natural when Dale decided to come on board with Merry Maids. He had a broad sales background and had just sold his carpet company; before that he'd had a cemetery business, so he was familiar with the dynamics of small businesses. My thought was to put him in charge of franchise sales in the Midwest region.

Dale ran an ad about Merry Maids in the St. Cloud, Minnesota, newspaper, and I flew into town to meet with him and a prospective owner. We had dinner together, and by the end of the evening the man had bought the St. Cloud franchise.

"This is just like the cemetery business," Dale told me dryly. "People are just dying to get in."

Dale started coming to Omaha every other week, participating with new owners in training classes. He'd sit across the desk from me while I'd talk with owners or make sales calls. We were working ten- to twelve-hour days, and he wasn't even a full-time employee yet.

One evening we went down the street for dinner after work. Dale has a great instinct for people and a keen ability to discern the ethos of a group of people or an organization.

"In every organization the leader sets the tone," Dale told me. "And you've set it here. There's something going on— much more than I had realized. The owners are really excited; they're committed to you and Glennis; they trust you, and there's a sense of momentum. You've got one heck of a business going here, and I don't think you even realize what's happening to you!"

"Well," I said, "I need you to come onboard with us full-time if we're going to grow this thing to its full potential."

And late in 1982 Dale did start to work full-time with us, handling all the franchise sales. He and I complemented one another well. Sometimes we seemed almost interchangeable; when needed, he was an extension of me, and it worked because we were twins. Other times we functioned in a good twin/bad twin kind of routine. As Dale puts it, I was the nice guy; he was willing to deal with the uncomfortable decisions I didn't want to face.

For example, during Dale's first week in the office, he had to fire my secretary. She had been an absolute disaster, but I had been too softhearted to ease her on her way into some other vocation for which she was more suited. But Dale saw that the person and the position were just not right for one another, and he took decisive action. When I returned from a franchise road trip, she was gone.

Over the years people sometimes wondered about the relationship between Dale and me. Was there tension or sibling rivalry between us?

Perhaps that's a normal expectation. But Dale and I respected one another, enjoyed one another, and understood one another on a very deep level. When we were growing up, he had typically been the dominant one in our relationship; in this business venture our roles had switched, and it was a new experience for both of us.

But in spite of the differences in our personalities, the pressures of the business, and our constant proximity to one another, I never felt any tension between us. I appreciated Dale's innate sense of confidence and his gift of candor! We would disagree on decisions occasionally—sometimes very vigorously—but we'd always come to agreement in the end because we were both committed to the same big-picture goals. Without Dale and his wife, Neola, Merry Maids wouldn't be where it is today.

Harlyn Brandt joined Merry Maids about the same time that Dale did. I had first met Harlyn back in the early 1970s at our church. He had just gotten his CPA; later he became our outside accountant for KAP's Foods. He was a quiet, reserved person who, of course, had a real gift for numbers; he had been one of our very first customers and joined us as our controller.

It was an exciting and natural decision to bring Dale and Harlyn on board, but it was also scary for me at the time. They both started at modest salaries, but they were a major addition to our home-office overhead. We were showing a profit at the time, but we were reinvesting everything back into the business, so there was little excess cash. I made sure every single payroll was met—except for a few times when I had to forego paying myself!

Without Dale and Harlyn, our growth would have been stymied. I simply could not have handled it.

But with them, we were off and running.

By the end of 1982 we had sold sixty-six franchises and were averaging one franchise sale every ten days. We were netting about $5,000 a month in profits—not a huge amount, of course, but we were on our way.

We continued to make our own line of cleaning products. They were of better quality than what was commercially available, were customized to our needs, and were priced to sell to our franchises at 10 percent over cost, or less. We weren't out to make money from our cleaning supplies. Our revenue would come from the 7 percent royalty fee our franchise owners paid to us. We didn't want to squeeze our owners on the small stuff; we wanted to empower them to succeed in the big stuff. If they did well, we would do well.

That's why we also took pride in filling orders for supplies the same day we received them. That immediate response told the franchise owners that we valued our relationship with them and that we empathized with them. We knew what it felt like to be a small business owner in need of supplies.

My greatest pleasure in the business was selling franchises. I've always loved people, and I passionately believed that the Merry Maids model could help them succeed. To me, selling franchises was a way of making financial success an attainable goal for people who were willing to work toward that end. And it was also a way to expand our corporate family.

Still, our sales efforts were low-key. The prospective owner would make the initial contact by phone or letter, and then we would proceed at his or her pace. Some people had already made up their minds and wanted to move quickly. Others needed a lot of time to weigh the pros and cons of the business. But whatever the pace, we wanted the people to know as much about Merry Maids as possible. We wanted them to know us inside and out and to feel absolutely comfortable with who we were. If they didn't trust us, there was no point in selling them a franchise.

With Dale on board, we were able to expand our sales significantly. Buyers had fun with the fact that we were identical twins. Sometimes they mixed us up, but the family aspect of the business was a powerful selling point. People could sense that if my twin brother and I were doing well, having fun, and hadn't killed each other, then they could do the same. We generally sold about a franchise a week, ending each year with about sixty to seventy-five new owners as part of the Merry Maids family.

Our sales materials were basic—no four-color photos or page after page of slick marketing copy. We wanted to keep it clean and simple. I knew that most prospective owners look into a dozen or more franchise opportunities, and I wanted our materials to be informative but quick to read. After all, cleaning homes is not rocket science; our brochures focused on the Merry Maids tools that could make an owner successful.

With prospective owners who were serious, I would set up

an appointment in their home rather than at a restaurant. That allowed me to get a better read on their interest, as well as their financial situation.

We didn't finance our franchises. It was in people's best interest, as well as ours, for them to make a complete financial commitment. Today many companies help to finance their franchise owners' costs. This may help sell franchises, but I'm not sure that owners who don't invest all their own capital—or don't have enough to buy on their own—make the commitment necessary to achieve a high degree of success.

Early on we also made the decision not to allow absentee ownership. Part of the Merry Maids culture—and our sense of energy and excitement—comes from owners actually running their own business and watching it grow.

Usually when couples would buy a franchise, one would work the business full-time, with the spouse working elsewhere and helping part-time for a while. After about six to twelve months—when sales would begin to increase dramatically—both would come onboard full-time.

In the early days, we would travel to meet with prospective owners, but as we got bigger and busier, we would invite potential owners to visit the home office. We would pay for half of their airfare and refund the other half if they bought a franchise. By this point we had competition in Omaha—The Maids, International—and they started doing the same thing. Some prospective owners would take advantage of both companies' programs. That was fine with us, but we always insisted that they visit us second. And I don't believe we ever lost a prospective owner to The Maids, International.

Visits by prospective owners were always announced to the

home-office staff in advance, and at least half of the staff participated in various aspects of the visit. That way, prospective owners could hear from a variety of personalities and perspectives on what the Merry Maids family was all about.

Franchises originally cost $5,000. Over the years that has risen to a range from $16,000 to $21,500. Owners who have successfully operated a franchise and then for one reason or another have decided to sell have realized great profits.

Today it's fairly common to see territories go for more than $300,000. And when a franchise is resold, Merry Maids treats and trains the buyer like any other new owner. We want the buyer to learn the business from us, not from the seller.

For most people, buying a franchise was a life-changing investment, and we wanted to be their partner in it. Many of the dynamics were like a marriage; the relationship involved commitment, trust, and good communications. And like any good marriage, good franchising takes a lot of work.

I knew that owning a small business can be a lonely experience. I wanted franchise owners to feel a strong sense of connection with our home office and that they were part of a team that supported them and cheered them on.

So, as I'll profile in detail in chapter 14, we developed as many useful communication tools as we could in order to strengthen those relationships and the owners' sense that they were part of a team, a family. To me, relationships are the key to business success, and you can't build good relationships without excellent communication skills.

But our greatest strides in the public-relations arena came through Tom Guy. Although Tom and I are very different personalities, we fit together well. We had worked together when

Tom was marketing manager at Fairmont Foods. (He'd dream up some wild product he wanted to market, and then I would have to figure out how to make it. Or I would produce some crazy snack that he'd have to figure out how to sell, like our famous Native American corn chips in the shape of arrowheads.)

At any rate, Tom and I had been good friends for years and had kept in touch often during Merry Maids' development. We had great creative camaraderie. By September 1984, with 165 franchises, I knew there was no one better than Tom to take Merry Maids to its next level of success—and that involved getting lots of media exposure to enhance our "brand name" recognition. So Tom was gracious enough to join us full-time as part of our executive team, which meant we also benefited from the support and insights of his wife, Letoi.

With Tom and Dale on board, I had strong expertise, strong opinions, and strong personalities to sharpen my own views. This was important: No matter how good my Merry Maids concept was or how much energy or expertise I poured into the company, I needed a strong team to lead this enterprise forward. No one person is multifaceted enough to carry a company to real long-term success. The key to growth and corporate health for the long run is for the vision-minded entrepreneur to surround himself or herself with talented people.

That's a basic fact, yet it surprises me how many talented executives surround themselves with yes men or intellectual inferiors in order to bolster their own egos or foster their own sense of job security.

So I felt that Merry Maids was really on its way in 1984, when our executive team of Dale, Tom, Harlyn, and me was in place. That was also the year that we began to entertain thoughts about franchising abroad. We had gotten a lot of press in America and had also been featured in the International Franchise Association publications. Entrepreneurs abroad were beginning to sense that we were on to something that could be replicated in their countries.

We began to explore that in the summer of 1984, when Glennis and I combined our vacation with a little bit of international networking. I made arrangements to visit with two businessmen—one in Germany, the other in France—who had contacted me about Merry Maids.

I soon realized that doing business in a foreign country was, in a word, foreign. Although Germany and France were similar to the U.S. in terms of such factors as the number of women employed outside the home and the number of middle-class and upper middle-class homes with disposable income for service industries, that's where the similarities ended.

In America, I had taken what is known as the Protestant work ethic for granted. In Europe, I saw that my ingrained assumptions about work didn't necessarily apply in foreign countries. I also found that my contacts in Europe were not very familiar with franchising or with the entrepreneurial spirit we Americans embrace. They didn't seem to appreciate the idea of franchise partners working together to enhance a company. And they did not have a sense of urgency or the zest and pressure that have both good and bad by-products in American business.

I felt that in many respects they were much more socialistic than in the U.S., particularly with socialized medicine, strong unions, and pay scales. Executives were not compensated that much more than the average worker, but unspoken fringe benefits were the accepted norm. For example, it was assumed that managers would arrive at the office much later and leave much earlier than the office staff and workers.

My first meeting was with a wealthy German businessman who owned several companies. He had traveled quite a bit in the U.S., so he was far more familiar with my culture than I was with his. But the Merry Maids concept of paying our service workers a percentage of each job—basically a commission—was utterly foreign to him.

"Why have we never thought of that?" he kept asking me.

I learned that German workers expected benefits like much more sick-leave time and more extensive holidays than our American workers do. Thus the costs of doing business were higher in Europe than in the U.S.

I realized that my German friend's interest was sincere but fairly superficial. And after my meeting in Bonn, I climbed on a train and left for Paris, where I had a dinner appointment with businessman Pierre Lefevre.

Now, I have traveled all over the world, both before and since my appointment with Monsieur Lefevre, but for some reason my thoughts were elsewhere when I left Bonn for Paris. I was thinking like an American and assumed that Paris, like most U.S. cities, had only one train station.

However, Paris has not one, but four train stations. Oblivious to that fact, I got off at the first station we came to.

Meanwhile my contact was expecting to meet me at the station on the opposite side of the city.

I strode through the station, surrounded by crowds of well-dressed Parisians who were chattering away in a language I could not understand, eyeing signs giving directions I could not decipher. I realized belatedly that it would have been wise to brush up on a few French phrases before I arrived. Just the basics. Like "Please," "Thank you," and *"Where in the world am I?"*

At last I saw an information kiosk in the distance. As I got closer, I saw to my great dismay a small sign that read, "Only French Spoken Here." I rushed to the booth in the vain hope that the three women inside might take pity on a lost midwesterner, but they looked me over and then made hand signals that made it clear they had no intention of speaking with this American.

I stopped various people in the crowd. No one could—or would—help me. I prayed—in English—and then God sent me a guardian angel. A beautiful middle-aged woman approached me and asked—in English—if she could be of assistance. I nearly kissed her hand.

My new friend explained that yes, I was in the wrong station on the wrong side of the city and that I had a good hour's train journey to get to my destination. She helped me buy my ticket, stayed with me on the train until she had to get off, and made sure that I knew to get off at #16. I felt like an immensely grateful kindergartner.

I arrived at the right station and made my way to the street where I was to meet Pierre. Within five minutes, a shiny black Jaguar swept up to the curb, and Pierre was at the wheel. I could have kissed him too.

Pierre spoke impeccable English. He was probably in his midforties, with gleaming black shoes, gray slacks, a checkered black-and-white jacket, and a bright yellow tie. He took me to an exquisite restaurant, and our conversation followed a similar pattern as my discussion with the German businessman.

Pierre had done his homework on cleaning services in the U.S. and had attended a franchise convention in Miami. He queried me at length about our training programs and asked if I could send him our video training tapes. Surely he knew we never let those into anyone's hands until they bought a franchise. I admired his chutzpah!

As we ate delicate French crêpes and sipped café au lait, we agreed that we would stay in touch and see what developed regarding Merry Maids in France.

Pierre had no idea how lost I was in his native city. After our meal, he dropped me off at the rail station. Waving, he sped away.

I then realized, belatedly, that I had made no hotel reservations in Paris and that it was now nearly midnight. I had learned no new French vocabulary words during dinner—and so here I was again, helpless in the train station!

I scanned the crowd. Weary travelers were sleeping on chairs, and a number of young people with backpacks were sitting on the floor, playing cards. I saw a young man wearing Reebok athletic shoes and carrying an L.L. Bean backpack, and I strode right toward him.

Eddie, a college student from Kansas City, had been traveling in Europe for three weeks and spoke enough French to get by. Eddie helped me buy a ticket to Brussels, where I could meet up with Glennis and the rest of the family. I settled into a six-passenger cabin and collapsed into exhausted slumber.

The next thing I knew, the conductor was tapping me on the shoulder, demanding my ticket. I gave it to him, and he burst into a torrent of angry French. I eventually gathered that I was in a first-class compartment but had paid only coach fare. Once I realized this, I kept shouting at him, "I'll pay the difference! I'll pay! I'll pay!"

Disgusted—and no more fluent in English than I was in French—he slammed the door and left. I stayed where I was and arrived, much the worse for wear, in Brussels at four o'clock in the morning.

Well, although these early adventures abroad seemed less than productive, the international relationships we cultivated in those early years eventually bore fruit. A truly good idea *can* be replicated in foreign countries; the model just needs to be adjusted to allow for cultural differences.

As I write, Merry Maids is licensed in Israel, Denmark, the United Kingdom, Japan, Canada, Australia, Chile, and Hong Kong.

Our strongest model abroad is in Japan, which probably offers the best example of adjusting the basic Merry Maids concept to allow for cultural differences.

Initially I was concerned about our name and how it would be interpreted in Japanese. I quickly learned, however, that American names are very important to the Japanese. All franchise companies, as well as well-known American brand names, are put at a premium in Japan. So Merry Maids retained its name and logo, although the Japanese did change our trademark yellow and green colors to pink and purple.

Our Japanese buyers did a tremendous amount of research into their new venture, sending ten of their staff people to Merry Maids headquarters in Omaha for a month of training. They left absolutely no stone unturned. They took extensive notes of every training class and every detail of our organization. They videotaped all of our techniques, from answering the phone to cleaning a kitchen, and they took hundreds of pictures of everything in between. I was extremely impressed by their courtesy and respect. And, since I'm a detail person myself, I loved their minute attention to detail!

Their diligence paid off. Today Merry Maids operates close to two hundred franchises in Japan, most of them in metropolitan areas.

As our experience in Japan illustrates, I knew the Merry Maids model would work abroad if it was tailored to the local culture. But for the most part, my focus was on the United States. I was most interested in developing our company at home, where I knew we had only begun to scratch the surface. I felt that greater and greater feats of success could be ours if we continued to serve our customers with our customary excellence—and continued to build relationships with more and more franchise owners.

And that certainly was the case. But my attention was also about to be diverted . . . by something I had never imagined would happen to me.

CHAPTER 9

Campaigns, Champagne, and Cardiac Pain

By the fall of 1985, the Merry Maids business was riding an exhilarating wave of success. We had just over 250 franchises coast to coast and continued to average about ten new franchise sales per month. We were receiving attention within the International Franchise Association and getting national publicity in a number of general media outlets as well.

To help us continue to grow, I had been thinking about buying a company airplane. I knew it would save us a lot of travel time since we wouldn't be dependent on airline schedules and delays, and it would allow us a lot more face time with potential franchise owners and existing owners.

We found a plane that we liked, a Beechcraft King Air, a nine-passenger turboprop jet. And the tough job of taking the luxury plane on a test flight fell to Glennis and me.

We flew with our pilot, Bert Aageson, to Denver and met our friends Bob and Carolyn Ellison for dinner. After a wonderful evening, Glennis and I climbed back aboard the plane, feeling quite content. We took off, angled over the mountains, and leaned back in the dark to enjoy the brilliant, star-studded skies.

We drifted gently off to sleep, . . . and then suddenly I
woke to a loud bang from the back of the plane. I looked out
and was not particularly reassured to see flames shooting out
of the left engine, right next to my window.

We didn't panic, though. I ran up to the cockpit and
strapped myself into the copilot's seat next to Bert. (I guess I
thought I could help there as well as anywhere.) Bert told me
we had been cleared for an emergency landing in North Platte,
Nebraska—about thirty-five miles away.

As we thundered down toward the runway, I saw what
seemed like every fire truck in the state down there waiting for
us, all with red lights swirling in the night. We landed hard
with just one engine, but the runway was long, and eventually
we came to a wobbling stop. Glennis, Bert, and I jumped off
the plane; emergency personnel were everywhere, but the fire
was out, and we were fine.

"Well, I don't think this is the plane for us," I told Glennis.

Later we did buy another plane, and it dramatically
changed the way we were able to follow up with franchise
prospects. I remember one of our first trips: Dale and I
started from Omaha, flew to the Quad Cities, then on to
Chicago. Dale stayed there while I went on to Maryland,
Washington, D.C., then back to Chicago to pick him up. We
returned home after two and a half days on the road—with
six new franchise sales!

Meanwhile, the exhilaration of our Merry Maids successes energized me for other endeavors as well. Although
I had not been particularly politically oriented in the past,
I had growing concerns about a number of the issues on our
state and national agenda. I believed that maybe I could help

make a difference in Nebraska's heavy tax burden, which was hurting the state's economy. Because of Nebraska's high corporate tax structure, our state was not appealing to outside companies.

So I found myself increasingly drawn toward politics—especially after I met the person who would become the next governor of our state.

I had first encountered Kay Orr in 1983, when she was state treasurer, the first woman in Nebraska to hold a statewide elected office. We met at a luncheon that was hosted by a friend and businessman, Bob Rhode. Bob and I had served on the local Prison Fellowship volunteer committee together, and Bob was helping Kay, who was from Lincoln, establish a network in Omaha.

I ended up sitting beside Kay, and I was struck by her insight, talent, and vision. And as Glennis and I spent more time with Kay and her husband, Bill, we also found that we had a lot in common in terms of our faith and our life perspectives.

Kay's belief in small business as a cornerstone for state growth also resonated with me. I began hosting small luncheons in our Merry Maids conference room, making them opportunities for Kay to meet a cross section of local Omaha businesspeople. In an informal setting, she could hear their concerns firsthand and respond in terms of her vision for what the state could—and should—be doing for its people. Kay's perspectives and her open attitude were particularly well received because Nebraska was at that time experiencing a period of apathy and stagnation under then-governor Bob Kerrey.

From my point of view, Kerrey's administration had not

been beneficial for Nebraska. He had cut spending, increased taxes, and invested little to move the state from a dying agricultural system to a more diversified economy. I welcomed his decision not to run again in 1986. So did the fifteen candidates who made the run for the primary election, including my friend Kay.

The national Republican party also encouraged Kay. She didn't have strong name recognition, but she received the most positive—and zero negative—ratings among the eight Republican candidates.

But raising funds for Kay was tremendously difficult. In spite of the national support, the local party bigwigs declined to contribute—I assume because the race was close and they didn't want to offend the seven other candidates.

I helped Kay assemble a grassroots campaign support group. We kicked off the campaign in November 1985 with a breakfast for the press and supporters in Omaha. Then we used our company plane to fly Kay to five different cities for a daylong series of campaign-announcement talks designed to showcase her all over the state.

Tom Guy and Jim Fowler, Merry Maids' marketing manager, had shown me how media exposure could benefit a business. One of Tom's greatest contributions was the way he consistently got Merry Maids in front of the public through news stories, television interviews, and print and radio features—for free. So I knew that media coverage was essential to the political process as well. The only problem was it was rather difficult to get positive political media exposure for free. You had to pay dearly for it.

So I did. Tom and Jim, along with Kay's ad agency, put

together a final few days' media strategy for the very last hours of the campaign. I was confident that a big push then, with plenty of strong political ads, could put Kay over the top. And when I called Kay on the campaign trail to tell her what we had done, she was so overwhelmed that she couldn't even talk. But her tears let me know just how much our backing meant.

It worked. Kay broke out of the pack to win the Republican primary. The Democratic victor was the mayor of Lincoln, Helen Bosalis. So our Nebraska general election became a national news story: it was the first time in history that two women ran against one another for a governorship in the United States.

Glennis and I continued in our support for Kay—and the fund-raising began in earnest. Money from the Republican bigwigs was no longer a problem, but I will say, without embellishment, that dealing with their egos was.

But still, I loved the competition and energy of the political game. And it was particularly exciting for me to get to know the national leaders who came to Nebraska to help Kay's effort.

Ronald Reagan, whom I have always deeply admired, made two Nebraska appearances for Kay in a two-month period. He wanted to make sure that our nation's first elected female governor was a Republican! I loved that Ronald Reagan's personal and private persona was no different from his public image: he was warm, friendly, and genuine. He loved to tell stories and had a remarkable sense of humor.

After months of effort, energy, planning, and prayer, election night arrived. I'll never forget the tension of waiting in the Holiday Inn as the district tallies came in, one by one.

The first numbers came in from Omaha, which is histori-
cally Democratic—so those results were of special interest to
us. We were five hundred votes ahead early in the evening, and
no one could remember that happening before for a Republican statewide candidate. And as the other districts' vote counts
began to come in, it appeared that Kay might well be the winner—but no one was ready to celebrate until the final tallies
were in. Kay, Glennis, and I felt the stress of a long campaign,
and we were anxious. The most confident person in our party
was Bill Orr, who had a keen political sense and a very strong
belief that he was going to be the first First Gentleman of
Nebraska.

And he was right.

We broke out the champagne as Kay Orr made history,
the first elected female Republican governor in the history
of the United States. It was exhilarating, not just because
she won, which is always a great feeling, but because I truly
believed that Kay represented the best political hope for the
people and businesses of Nebraska.

In the euphoria of Kay's victory, I agreed to cochair the
inaugural ball. So the next thing I knew, we were throwing
a party for fourteen thousand friends, including a sit-down
dinner for three thousand people. It was a major event for
Nebraska, particularly since a number of key Washington
politicians attended. They saw in Kay a future political star
who had potential on the national level.

Shortly after Kay took office, the Democratic senator from
Nebraska died of a heart attack. It was up to Kay to appoint
his replacement. It was an unexpected challenge, an important
decision, and Kay wrestled with a number of possibilities.

After a grueling few days, she selected a young political unknown: an Omaha attorney and businessman named Dave Karnes. Dave represented everything that Kay believed could best serve the people of Nebraska: he was a political outsider, not beholden to any special-interest groups; he had immutable convictions about the dignity of human life and commitment to help those who could not help themselves; and he was a person of unshakable character and absolute integrity.

Dave's most ardent supporters were his wife, Liz, and his four young daughters. Liz was a particularly strong political spouse; she had her Ph.D. in education and had been supervisor of curriculum and instruction at Boys Town for twelve years.

However, all this did not impress the distinguished members of the media. They went crazy and gave Kay a horrendous time about choosing an unknown Puritan prude.

The second challenge Kay Orr faced as governor occurred when the president of ConAgra threatened to move his company out of Nebraska; this was shortly after another major corporation, Enron, had left the state. Kay handled the tough situation masterfully. She was able to get a strong economic-development package through the unicameral chamber (the only single-house legislature in the country). The legislation's tax benefits produced hundreds of millions in new business investment in Nebraska—and thousands of new jobs.

Kay proved to be a strong state leader, and Glennis and I were proud to have served on her election team. Although she did not win her second term—in part because of a blizzard on election day that kept many Third District Republicans away from the polls—she served Nebraska well.

Today, all these years later, we are working together again—but now as members of Prison Fellowship's board of directors. It's exhilarating to be able to effect real change in people's lives—offenders, their families, the victims of crime—without being held hostage to the idiosyncrasies of the political process.

I enjoyed it while it lasted.

At any rate, my foray into politics in the late 1980s fit with the other aspects of my life in that I enjoyed the hard work, the challenge, the outpouring of energy.

But in that, I was moving at a speed that was hazardous to my health. I was like a lot of American businesspeople. I raced from meeting to meeting. My calendar was a whirlwind of commitments. At home, Glennis ran a tight ship, as usual, but we were both very busy with franchise training dinners, charitable events, church meetings, and a host of other engagements, stresses, and pressures. These things were all good—but I was overloaded. I just didn't realize it. I felt fine. I loved what I was doing.

But then God nudged me to reassess my priorities by rocking my boat ever so slightly. I'm just grateful he didn't allow it to capsize!

It was a breezy Saturday night in April. Glennis and I had just returned from a hectic trip to California, where we were meeting with a number of Merry Maids franchise owners. We got home in time to jump into our formal clothes; we were serving as cochairs of a charitable event that evening at our son's private school.

At the gala, we chatted with friends, smiled, toasted, posed for photos, had a great time. But by the end of the night I was uncharacteristically tired. We drove home just before mid-night. I was flushed and perspiring a bit.

The next morning, as we sat in our usual pew at church, I began to feel dizzy and numb around my upper body and shoulders. Sweat poured down my chest. We left the service, and Glennis took me to the emergency room at Methodist Hospital. The doctor there checked me over and sent me home.

By late afternoon, however, I knew something was very wrong. We went back to the hospital—and the next thing I knew I was in cardiac intensive care, tubes emerging from all over my body and computer screens monitoring my every function. I'd had a heart attack.

I was very fortunate: it was minor. But this reminder of my mortality—not to mention my advancing age—dismayed me. Then the doctor prescribed my ongoing treatment, which also confounded me: complete bed rest, four weeks away from the office, and a sharply curtailed schedule when I returned.

I had always known that our executive-committee form of management at Merry Maids was wonderfully sound. But in the weeks after my heart attack, I saw just how good it was. Dale, Harlyn, and Tom kept the company running smoothly. I thought that if there had been video screens monitoring Merry Maids' health the same way they had tracked my health at the hospital, those monitors never would have shown the slightest dip at my absence. New sales, franchise relations, and profitability continued to soar. It was clear that Merry Maids could be merry without me.

As you've perceived in this book, I'm not a particularly reflective person. I like action. I like people. I don't enjoy being still or alone. But in the recuperation period following my heart attack, God gave me a mandatory sabbatical. And in that forced solitude, I took stock in a way I could not during my usual frenetic schedule.

First, I realized again the wonderful priority of family. For some strange reason, it seems to be human nature to take those we love most for granted. But as I convalesced and watched Glennis and our five children, their spouses, and their children all hanging around my bed, laughing and teasing, I thanked God in a fresh way for the amazing blessing of my family.

Second, as I mentioned, I felt so grateful for my colleagues at Merry Maids. They sent more than one hundred flower arrangements to the hospital—tangible reminders of our relationships. I've always valued people, so it wasn't as if I had taken my coworkers for granted. But the heart attack caused me to realize in a fresh way the absolute *privilege* of good, hard work with gifted, creative colleagues. I thought about the challenges, the laughter, the meetings in which we had knocked our heads together to find the best ways to see our business grow. Some people work for a lifetime without ever enjoying that kind of productive, energizing camaraderie.

And third, although I mentioned it rather facetiously earlier, my heart attack really did cause me to think about my own mortality. Because of my faith in Christ and the power of his grace, I felt confident about where I would spend eternity. But what about the rest of life here on this earth?

I'm forty-nine years old, I thought. *Only God knows how many more years are left. How do I use them in the best way possible?*

CHAPTER 10

The $25 Million Dinner

By June of 1987, I was back at work full-time, feeling strong again but trying to establish new, healthier habits. In fact, I had my own personal health police: Glennis and the children monitored me constantly. Every time I ate a donut or pushed myself too hard, they were all over me.

Merry Maids continued to grow and prosper. And late that year, a company that was interested in buying Merry Maids quietly approached me. The company was a well-known manufacturer of homecleaning products; they were well established and financially solid.

Since the heart attack, I had thought about trimming my schedule, and even somewhere in the back of my mind I had entertained the possibility of selling the company. But I loved Merry Maids and couldn't quite imagine letting it go.

Still, Glennis and I accepted an invitation to visit the company's corporate headquarters. There we were wined and dined in quite elegant fashion, but I had no gut sense that this was a match made in heaven or anywhere else. I just didn't see the synergy between our companies. It also seemed to me that their interests lay in finding new distribution channels for their housecleaning products, not in the continued growth and development of Merry Maids.

But the acquisition opportunity did cause me to have an independent assessment done of Merry Maids' worth. I hired an appraisal company to estimate our worth in the event of a sale, which I absolutely was not planning.

All that changed in the course of a weekend.

Oddly—or perhaps, appropriately enough—the sale of a lifetime began in prison.

It was Good Friday, 1988. Chuck Colson was planning to conduct Prison Fellowship services in four prisons in Nebraska and Iowa, and I had offered to accompany him and have our plane fly him between prisons that day.

The prisoners we met that day were very similar to the men I had drawn close to during my Bible study behind bars. There was a mix of Caucasian, African-American, and Native American. Most were in their twenties; some looked like teenagers. I felt that any could have been my son.

As always, Chuck established an immediate rapport with the men. In spite of his former political power and prestige— with which these men could not relate—they saw him not only as a fellow felon but also as a man who had decided to follow Christ and who genuinely cared for them.

As a result, the prisoners were very open to Chuck's message. I thought, as I have so often since, that there's no place I would rather be on Easter than in prison: the church behind the barbed wire has a vitality and openness that is sometimes hard to find on the outside.

After the service, we hugged and shook hands with

as many inmates as we could, then took off for our next destination, ascending through rather thick cloud cover toward Des Moines. Chuck Colson is one of the most focused people I've ever met; he does not spend much time in idle conversation.

"Well, Dallen," he said, turning toward me, "you've come through a heart attack. You know life is short. What do you plan to be doing five years from now—assuming you're still around?"

"I'm thankful," I said slowly. "I can't believe how well Merry Maids has done. I never expected this kind of financial success."

But even as I said those words, I was questioning whether I had hit a plateau. Maybe the old energy and momentum weren't there for me anymore, even though the company was doing well. Perhaps I wasn't driving toward new challenges.

"I don't know," I responded to Chuck. "Maybe I'll sell Merry Maids and work with you!"

Chuck laughed, but I could see the wheels turning inside his head. Then we descended into Des Moines for the next prison service.

That was the end of it—for about seventy-two hours.

The next evening Chuck and Patty Colson had dinner in Florida with their old friends Ken and Norma Wessner. Ken was a member of Prison Fellowship's board of directors.

Chuck called me the next morning. "Dallen," he said, "I hope I didn't betray your confidence last evening, but I mentioned to Ken Wessner that you might be interested in selling Merry Maids. He was intrigued by the idea and couldn't wait to get to the phone."

"Who's Ken Wessner?" I asked.

"He's chairman of the board of ServiceMaster," Chuck told me.

I was familiar with ServiceMaster. I knew about their carpet-cleaning services and had also had a little experience with their disaster-relief services back when a local ServiceMaster franchise had come in to restore our cupboards and clean up the damage from a fire we'd had in our home.

I knew a little about the company's foundations as well: unlike many corporations, whose mission statements are simply nice phrases that adorn their annual reports, ServiceMaster deliberately incorporated its mission into its day-to-day operations. That mission sprang from the Christian commitment of its founders.

ServiceMaster's founder, Marion Wade, had started a small mothproofing company during the depression. A few years later, enjoying modest success, he expanded into carpet-cleaning. Temporarily sidelined by a work-related chemical accident, Wade took a fresh look at his life's priorities and practices. He recommitted himself to God's service and dedicated his business to God.

By 1947 Marion Wade had established a long-term partnership with Ken Hansen, a friend who shared his spiritual perspective and the priority of honoring God in all of one's daily affairs, no matter how mundane. Five years later Wade's company sold its first franchise, and by 1957 the company's franchises were operating under the slogan: "masters of service, serving the Master."

In 1961 the company, with Marion Wade as chairman and Ken Hansen as president, changed its name to ServiceMaster.

The next year its stock went public. I had known it was a solid presence in the market; in fact, I had always included some ServiceMaster stock as part of my investment portfolio. Little did I know the eventual role that stock would play in my life.

It wasn't too long after I hung up from talking with Chuck that I received a call from Bill Pollard, ServiceMaster's president and CEO. I soon learned that Ken, Bill, and ServiceMaster were extremely interested in acquiring a maid-service company.

ServiceMaster had bought the pest-control company Terminix in 1986, and the parent company was interested in branching out into a variety of other aspects of the home-service industry market.

In fact, also in 1986, ServiceMaster developed its own homecleaning business, HomeBright. But by 1988 it was clear that HomeBright was not growing as fast as they wanted it to.

ServiceMaster had seen our energetic growth, and since we were number one in the homecleaning field, the ServiceMaster leadership was now very interested in the entire Merry Maids operation.

But the link between ServiceMaster and Merry Maids began with more than mere financial attraction. Our core philosophies merged as well. The Judeo-Christian worldview that undergirded both our companies served as the foundation of our shared business values and practices.

I was astonished to discover that ServiceMaster's corporate objectives were the same—almost word for word—as Merry Maids' goals. As Ken Wessner had refined and focused them, the company's purposes were to honor God, to help people grow, to pursue excellence, and to grow profitably.

If there was ever a marriage that would benefit Merry

Maids' core values and the people who held them—the *soul* of our firm, as Bill Pollard called it—this was it. The potential sale would be more than a financial contract. It would be a union of hearts, intents, and vision for the future.

Maybe, I thought, *God really* is *leading me to sell this company.* But I was uncertain. I didn't know what would truly be best for the company and our people at that time. I sensed the tremendous synergy between Merry Maids and ServiceMaster. But I doubted that any corporation could run Merry Maids with the same personal focus that we had.

And I knew that our family would be somewhat skeptical of a big change. Everyone had been involved with our growth in one way or another. At that time our daughter Kim had a franchise in Kansas City, Kris's husband was working in sales, Brian was working in operations, and Dale was vice president of sales. I knew they would all be affected in one way or another.

But still, I knew ServiceMaster had incredible potential to help Merry Maids grow as a company and help its people develop. I prayed about the decision all the time, that God would give Glennis and me wisdom to do the right thing.

In May, Glennis and I flew to Chicago to meet with Bill Pollard and see ServiceMaster's operations firsthand. It was then that I met Ken Wessner, ServiceMaster's chairman of the board.

I found Ken to be the ideal Christian businessman: a person of integrity, humility, and wisdom. We were physical opposites: Ken was tall and lanky; I am short and compact. But we related to one another on many levels. We both were entrepreneurs at heart and liked to venture into new things.

Our common interest in Prison Fellowship and our mutual friendship with Chuck Colson drew us together as well. Ken's caliber as a human being, a businessman, and a mentor drew me strongly toward ServiceMaster. He became a friend and a mentor—for life.

Meanwhile, in spite of my heart-healthy pledge, my weekly schedule was unusually hectic. When I look back, I get tired just looking at my diaries and logs from the spring of 1988. I was heavily involved in state politics, overseeing Dave Karnes's campaign for the United States Senate, flying all over the state as I managed finances, staff, PR, and everything else. As usual, Dale, Tom, and Harlyn were running a tight ship at Merry Maids, but I was still very busy there.

And meanwhile I was engaged in confidential, sensitive meetings and negotiations with ServiceMaster.

By June, the corporate assessment I had contracted was complete, just about the time that ServiceMaster's accountants concluded their own investigation. Our analysts told me that they put Merry Maids' worth at $25–$27 million.

Hmmm, I thought. *Not bad for eight years' work.*

By this point, Glennis and I had decided together that what we really wanted was not our own agenda, but *God's* will. We weren't sure if he wanted us to sell our company or keep it. We had a lot of strong feelings about keeping it, but we also had a sense that the time might be right to sell, especially given the wake-up call of my heart attack.

We prayed continually. Just as we had before we launched Merry Maids, we wanted to put our trust in God—and let *him* direct our paths.

Then Bill Pollard called to say that he was flying from

Chicago to Omaha. Could we meet and have dinner together? He had talked with his board of directors, and he was ready to make us an offer.

I appreciated the way Bill was courting us. Although a team of accountants and attorneys had become a necessary part of the formalities, what we were building here was a relationship of mutual trust and respect. It felt more like an alliance than an acquisition, more like a marriage than a merger. And so it felt appropriate that we were meeting with Bill over a meal, just the three of us.

As we drove toward the airport to pick Bill up on that fresh June evening, Glennis asked, "Well, what are we going to do?"

"I'm not sure," I told her. "But if his proposal is at all close to the appraised value we've been given, I think that could well be a sign from God."

I had arranged for a corner table at the Plaza Club. Candles glowed, and we could smell the light fragrance of the fresh roses in their vase on the snowy white, starched tablecloth. While we ate our rack of lamb and big Omaha steaks, we talked about our businesses. Merry Maids had had another blockbuster month in May, with nine franchise sales. Bill was very interested in that.

When coffee and dessert came, Bill leaned toward me. He reached into his jacket pocket and pulled out a single sheet of paper, folded crisply in half, lengthwise. He passed it to me, and for a second I just stared at it. *They're probably going to come in very low,* I thought. *Standard negotiating practice.*

Then I opened it.

There were five or six items, listed in short order.

The first item leaped out at me: "ServiceMaster proposes to purchase the assets of Merry Maids from Dallen and Glennis Peterson, for $25 million."

Oh! I thought. *I guess they're serious.*

I passed the paper to Glennis. She read it and spent the next ten minutes or so trying to locate her eyeballs, which had popped out somewhere near her dessert plate.

"Well," I said to Bill. "This is an offer we'll have to consider seriously." Bill knew I wasn't interested in negotiating, that I would take or leave his offer. And I knew that no matter how good I felt about this deal, it wasn't truly a deal until all the papers had been signed and the money exchanged. So I found myself in a curious blend of caution and exultation.

Bill told me that ServiceMaster would not make any big changes at Merry Maids and that they wouldn't move the company from Omaha. He also asked me if I would stay on.

"If that's one of the conditions," I told him, "then I won't sell." I knew that I needed either to own the company and run it or to move on. I had had my experience in corporate life. Now I was too independent to go back.

"All right," Bill said. "The other thing is, if you're interested, we would like to close by June 30."

My eyebrows went up at that. June 30 was just over three weeks away. I told Bill I would call my attorney in the morning.

As the lovely evening at the Plaza Club ended, Bill and I shook hands, and then he gave Glennis a quick hug.

If you had seen Glennis and me driving home that night, you would have thought we were returning from either a funeral or a particularly boring movie. We hardly spoke. I think we were both numb.

Although it was a consolation to have each other and to feel as if we were looking to God for leadership, this was also one of the loneliest periods in my life. I've always bounced ideas off of other people; I've always sought wisdom, perspectives, and reactions from others. But here we were, in the midst of one of the biggest decisions of our lives, and we had to keep it to ourselves.

But both Glennis and I had a sense of God's clear leading, and as the days went by, our discussions with ServiceMaster turned from issues of if and why to when and how.

Around this time Bill mentioned that ServiceMaster wanted me in the role of a senior advisor to the board. I told him, "You're moving so quickly in all this! You don't really even know me."

He said, rather mysteriously, "Well, Dallen, we know more about you than you think."

Bill's remark affirmed what I was feeling inside. Successful business deals have a lot more to do with the pull of the gut and shared life perspectives than they do with the numbers on the balance sheets. That's because businesses are run by human beings, not bloodless computers. And as long as that is true, *relationships* are the most important component.

But there were a lot of other relationships to tend to as well. In mid-June I traveled to Canada for the annual "male-bonding" fishing weekend with our sons Brian and Brett, our son-in-law George, Greg Hase, Rollie Schwery, Gary Veuve, and Gene McNamara.

As I sat in the fishing boat I shared with Gene, on the hunt for walleyes and lake trout, I felt as if I would burst if I didn't let him know what was happening. We had been close confidants since 1964. Gene had had one of our first franchises; I didn't want him to feel that I was betraying him. I was surprised at how nervous I felt about telling my old friend of the decision Glennis and I had made.

Sitting in the fourteen-foot boat, our lines in the water, I cleared my throat. "Gene," I said, "I've got something important to tell you."

He looked at me suspiciously, as if Glennis and I were going to have another baby, or I had decided to join the Peace Corps.

"I've decided to sell Merry Maids," I said flatly.

I thought Gene was going to fall out of the boat. We rocked in the water for a moment, and then he sputtered, "Who?"

"ServiceMaster," I said.

"Why?" he said, seemingly unable to get out words of more than one syllable.

"Well," I said, feeling ridiculous, "they're very interested in maid service, it's a good company, and I'm pretty impressed.

"They're very serious," I added lamely, thinking about the $25 million offer already on the table.

After Gene recovered and we talked about all the benefits the sale could mean for the people of Merry Maids, who were my chief concern, Gene became slightly more comfortable with the idea. And it helped me tremendously to have been able to talk about it with a friend. Gene agreed to keep it in confidence. I knew that our conversation would stay private, and it did.

It was more difficult the following week when I told Dale and Tom.

They were in shock, but within a few days they rallied to put together a package in order to buy me out. But it was too late. I told them I had already signed a binding letter of intent with ServiceMaster, and I could not change that. I had to fulfill my commitment.

Also, I didn't want the entire Merry Maids staff to be exposed to a period of uncertainty. My thought had been that if the ServiceMaster deal fell through, then that would happen privately, and no one would have gone through unnecessary anxiety. But if the staff knew that the business was for sale and that Dale and Tom were trying to buy me out, but it wasn't a done deal, then they would be launched on an emotional roller coaster. If the ServiceMaster deal worked out, then it would be a one-time surprise: difficult to deal with initially, perhaps, but a solid decision, already made.

And at the bottom line, I truly believed that ServiceMaster offered Merry Maids growth opportunities that would take our owners and staff to a whole new level of success. Service-Master's financial health as an organization and its spiritual health as a business that put God first would be good for the Merry Maids family.

As the ServiceMaster negotiations drew to a close, we were all amazed at how smoothly the transaction was completed. Bill Pollard and I had agreed from the beginning that we wanted to keep our lawyers busy on the necessary business aspects of the agreement—but that we wanted the heart of the deal to be built on a relationship of common trust, respect, and integrity.

Toward that end, I made sure that our resource center was fully stocked, ready to be handed over with a high level of inventory. I told Bill that we would pay all of our bills up to the date of closing. ServiceMaster would assume everything the day after closing. And the level of trust between us was such that Bill simply agreed; ServiceMaster didn't check the inventory or police our bills. And for my part, everything was done as we said it would be.

We signed and closed our deal on July 5, 1988. Glennis, Dale, Harlyn, and I flew to Chicago for the ceremony, and Tom stayed back in Omaha to churn out the press releases.

Soon after we returned, we embarked on a blitz trip to Merry Maids offices around the country. I took the company plane and went to Seattle, Oakland, Los Angeles, Phoenix, Denver, Kansas City, Dallas, Birmingham, Tampa, Baltimore, Philadelphia, Boston, Detroit, Chicago, Minneapolis, and back to Omaha. In each of those cities, I sat down with local and regional Merry Maids staff to tell them personally how I had come to this decision. I knew that rumors of every kind would fly, so I thought it best to talk face-to-face with as many people as I could.

I also knew I couldn't make everything easy and tidy for them. It was going to mean change, and people don't usually respond well to change—especially changes initiated by others. But I believed that they would see the immense benefits of being part of ServiceMaster and know that the change was for their good. I also knew that the relationships we had cultivated over the years were strong enough to withstand the winds of change.

I attended my first ServiceMaster board meeting the week after my whirlwind tour of the nation. I was deeply impressed with the caliber and experience of the other board members. I felt I could learn a lot from them.

By August, Glennis and I knew we needed to get away. We needed to process the huge changes that had come upon us and spend some time together alone. We flew to Juneau and boarded a Dutch liner for a cruise of the Alaskan coast.

After the unusually hot, dry Omaha summer, the gentle days and cool nights were immensely refreshing to us. So, after we got used to it, we actually relaxed.

We watched as whales cavorted in the water; we relaxed in deck chairs as the golden sun set each evening. We held our breath in the stillness as enormous, ancient glaciers crashed from peaks high above the bay and tumbled into the water. In a slow-motion reaction, after the tons of ice would drop, our ship would rock in the water—two miles away.

Often, as I watched the last rays of the sun slip from the broad Alaskan sky, I thought about the sale of Merry Maids— the years of work, the risks and joys and friendships, the daily challenges of the business.

Because of the ServiceMaster sale, enormous changes had come. We had gained immeasurably. But there was loss as well. Like those big glaciers, it was as if big parts of our lives were dropping away, and I could not help but wonder if the resulting waves would rock our boat.

Full Circle

Selling Merry Maids brought one of the most exciting, fulfill-
ing chapters of our lives to a conclusion. Glennis and I were
confident it was the right step to take. At the same time, it was
hard for us to give up the company we had started. And it was
painful to pull away from the people who had become a family
to us—not to mention all of our relatives who were involved
with Merry Maids as well!

Those ties went deep. It was as if Glennis and I had given
birth to a baby that had grown and grown and grown. Even
though that baby was going off and getting married, we were
still its parents, watching it fondly, worrying a little, telling ourselves to pull back so it could enjoy its next season of growth.

Bill Pollard had invited me to stay on as president. But
as much as I respected Bill, ServiceMaster president Carlos
Cantu, and the ServiceMaster company itself, I knew that
corporate life was not for me.

To grow in its new context, Merry Maids would need to
find the right balance of retaining its unique identity while
assimilating into its parent company's corporate culture. In

spite of the fact that Bill had reassured our franchise owners and home office that there would be no substantive changes (except for aspects like insurance and other technical revisions), I knew that change was inevitable. And as long as I was around, it would be hard for the Merry Maids team to embrace those changes in a healthy way.

The first month after the sale was hard. Contractually, I was no longer bound, but to try to help ease the transition, I came to the home office each morning. I moved out of my corner office and took a smaller office in the executive wing, gradually disengaging so our staff could develop relationships with the new leadership.

Many franchise owners and staff members were wary. They felt, understandably, that Merry Maids had long been the leader in our industry and that they knew a lot more than ServiceMaster did about the housecleaning business. For weeks, Dale and Tom handled countless phone calls from all over the country, reassuring our people that Merry Maids' greatest days were still ahead, that ServiceMaster would provide opportunities we could never see on our own. And these things have proven to be true. But still, human nature being what it is, the change was hard for everyone.

As often happens in businesses or other institutions, the acting president who took over from the founder did not stay long. The man who followed me as president had a distinguished history as a gifted corporate executive. But in his early days at Merry Maids, he made at least two false assumptions.

First, I believe that he took one of Merry Maids' key institutional strengths for granted: the tremendous priority of relationships and the deep-seated loyalty owners and staffers had toward me. Perhaps he assumed it was loyalty to the *office* of president. But it was actually a commitment and trust built on the years that I had invested in all those relationships, the priceless personal ties that had bound our company together. He seemed to assume that that loyalty would automatically transfer to him. But it did not. It would have to be earned.

But that was not to be because he did not seem to understand the second key component of Merry Maids' identity.

Long trained as a corporate executive, my successor didn't discern the differences between standard line management and the complexities of managing a franchise business. Franchise owners need to feel part of the decision-making process. They have an extremely high need for communication, one that is increased by the fact that they're isolated, scattered all over the country in small, storefront offices. And our franchise owners' involvement was much more visceral than that of nine-to-five employees: they had invested their hard-earned dollars to become part of the company.

Far more significant, they had also invested their own sweat equity. In the early days of their franchises, many owners had cleaned houses, answered phones, washed cleaning rags, and repaired vacuum cleaners—anything, no matter how menial—to keep their fledgling businesses afloat.

And we had invested in them. We had spent hours with them during their training days at the home office. They had dined in our home; they had scrutinized our bedroom and bathroom, inch by inch, when we trained them how to do estimates. They had laughed with our children and met our grandchildren. I had been in touch with many of them to congratulate them on their own milestones: business goals attained, wedding anniversaries, the births of their children.

For these owners, Merry Maids was not just a corporate enterprise. They didn't consider themselves employees or investors. They thought of themselves as family, and they were used to my way of doing things.

So my successor experienced difficulties from the start. Unfamiliar with our company ethos and assuming the loyalty people felt toward me would transfer to him, he did not build his own relationships with our home-office staff and our franchise owners. Business and growth were affected.

A transition president, Don Parkhurst, was brought in. Don had served as ServiceMaster's managing director in the UK and was ready to lead Merry Maids by learning. I worked with him behind the scenes and began to feel that the company was on its way to new heights.

So I hoped that great things were ahead for "our baby." I also realized that I needed to remove myself from the scene so it could grow in new ways.

Omaha is a small city, and I had a high profile there. Right after the sale our pictures were in all the newspapers and all over the nightly news—"the $25 million sale." People would stop Glennis and me on the street. Many were interested in financial help of one kind or another. And everyone asked us about Merry Maids.

So Glennis and I decided to move back to our family roots in Minnesota. Our home in Omaha sold in two days. I had always liked its design, and I'm the type of person who feels that if something's not broken, why fix it. So we built the identical house on the banks of Norway Lake in Minne-

sota, a few hundred yards from the old farmhouse where
I was born.

The house was finished in the spring of 1989. As we moved
in, I felt I had come full circle. The man with the briefcase was
back to his country roots.

I soon fell into familiar routines. I'd walk the cornfields—
now harvested by someone else—with my father. On Saturday
mornings I'd sit in my mother's kitchen—fifteen feet from the
room where I was born—and eat Mom's biscuits and bacon
as Dad would meticulously fry one egg at a time, over easy.

Just as in my childhood, I'd be surrounded by brothers
and sisters who were laughing, joking, and giving one
another—especially me—a hard time. But now the family
was bigger, with spouses and grandchildren crowding around
as well. Most Saturdays, Mom would feed at least ten people,
always urging us to eat a little more, try some peach pre-
serves, have another piece of toast.

Within a few years, other family and friends joined us.
Dale built a home next door to ours, and my cousin Evy and
her husband, Paul, moved in down the road. Our son Brett and
his family were nearby, and my sisters Linda and Renita and
brother Jim already lived in Willmar, a few miles away. My old
friend Gene McNamara built a summer home five doors up
from us.

Glennis developed a love of quarter horses, and in my
usual enthusiasm, I bought several of them. We built a beautiful stable across the road from our home. Glennis would
be over there every morning by seven o'clock, greeting the
horses—as well as miscellaneous kittens that were always
multiplying in the barn—and mucking out the stalls.

Our stables also happened to have the cleanest water supply in the community, so most evenings our neighbors and family would stop by the barn to restock their fresh drinking water. It was like the local well in a small village. We would fill up our water containers and fill each other in on the day's news, while Pidge, our golden retriever, chased the kittens and played with my cousin's collie.

In the winters we would take our kids and the growing tribe of grandchildren snowmobiling and ice fishing. In the summers we would skim over the waters of Norway Lake—where I had almost drowned so many decades earlier—in our boat.

Every morning, I'd drive into New London—population 971—for coffee with "the boys." In the tradition of small-town people everywhere, we'd solve the world's problems right there at the Formica-topped tables of the Hillcrest Restaurant. My friends there were carpenters, construction workers, a railroader, even a junk dealer. Just listening to them was a sharp contrast from the stresses of running a nationwide company—but it kept my perspectives in focus. So did Friday evenings at the American Legion hall, where Glennis and I would go to eat a fried walleye dinner and listen to a local band.

So our lives after selling Merry Maids were a little bit like those of people in Mayberry. It was a great blessing to have the *time* that money makes possible. Time to enjoy the slower rhythms of small-town life. Time with our children, grandchildren, and friends.

We also had time to give to charitable work and various ministries. I took on a number of board memberships, feeling that I could help organizations like Prison Fellowship, Luther Seminary, and Waldorf College with some of the principles that I had learned through Merry Maids.

Selling Merry Maids also meant that we had the financial resources available to give generously to causes we believed in. Ever since Glennis and I became committed Christians, we had always tithed—given 10 percent of our income—to ministries, missions, and our church. We continued that and also were able to expand our giving toward causes that were close to our hearts.

One cause, of course, was prison ministry. I've been going into prisons for more than twenty-five years now, and it's been a great blessing to be able to give generously to Prison Fellowship. It's been rewarding to know that thousands of lives are being changed, one at a time, through the power of God. Just as I had the privilege of participating in the lives of prisoners like Mel Goebel and Rick Sendgraff so many years ago, now I'm able to help support thousands of Prison Fellowship volunteers every day who go to do the same.

But having money and being retired isn't just about giving resources to help facilitate *other* people's ministries. Glennis and I were determined that our wealth would not isolate us from helping people firsthand.

For example, Glennis has done short-term relief work in an elementary school in the Dominican Republic. Serving as an amateur dental hygienist, she helped to clean and condition the teeth of more than fifty young children. She also held them, rocked them, and brought them clothes and supplies to help make their lives easier. Their situation was very difficult, but Glennis entered into it. Since then we've sponsored a medical doctor to go to the school once a week, and we're supporting two of the children.

I think of opportunities like that when I say that the years since our $25 million dinner with Bill Pollard have been rich indeed. I don't mean monetarily, although of course we've been financially blessed beyond our wildest dreams.

I mean we've become rich in the things that *really* matter.

That's why selling Merry Maids and achieving financial security is not the end of our story. In many ways, it's just the beginning!

CHAPTER 12

Real Success

I remember when Glennis and I were in our early twenties, living with our three young children in a two-bedroom apartment. We had nothing in our savings account, nothing in the stock market, and we lived from paycheck to paycheck. Money was very tight.

But I remember how very good it was when we had a little extra on a summer evening, and we would buy a gallon of chocolate ice cream from the market down the street. We would invite the neighbors, break out our best plastic spoons, and make it an event. Life was good!

Today I have assets I could not have imagined back in those sticky summer evenings in 1963. But I still can't think of a greater pleasure than breaking out the ice cream and laughing with the neighbors.

That's because selling Merry Maids was not the pot of gold at the end of the rainbow for Glennis and me. It did not change who we are or what we enjoy. Of course we will always be immensely grateful for the great blessing of financial success—but that, in itself, was not the goal.

Selling Merry Maids in the summer of 1988 was just a station along the way in our lives. We're still the same people. We have not forgotten where we came from or what our parents taught us. And the challenge now, as always, is for Glennis and me to be good stewards of what we've been given. Our economic situation doesn't determine our priorities in life; those values remain the same whether we have much or we have little.

And in this season when we have much, we know that money alone will never satisfy. What counts is how it is used for others—in fact, how it is used for *eternal* purposes.

Over the last few years, as I've looked at the books that ascend to the top of America's best-seller lists, I've noticed that many seem to ignore this fact. There are lots of books out there about how to get rich and climb the corporate ladder. There are lots of happy success stories about businesspeople who grabbed that brass ring.

If that were all that our story was about, it wouldn't be worth writing—or reading. But I believe that our story does have something different to offer. In it I want to pass on seven principles that can help you do well financially. But that's not enough. It is far more important to learn to live well spiritually, to apply the principles of deep and lasting success in life and relationships.

Many of the books I've seen in the marketplace seem to ignore the very basic fact that wealth alone does not bring happiness, fulfillment, or *real* security. In fact, wealth alone often brings its own name brand of well-heeled misery.

Having hit the big time, many people discard the spouses who stood with them through the lean years. Many men soothe their fading physical vigor with young trophy wives who might love them just for their portfolios, not their personalities! Many people lose touch with their children. Many leave old friends behind as they upgrade to wealthier peers. Many try to fill their spiritual emptiness with material assets.

Such poverty among the rich is tragic. As it says in the Bible, "How do you benefit if you gain the whole world but lose your own soul in the process? Is anything worth more than your soul?" (Matt. 16:26, NLT).

As human beings, we all know intrinsically that this life is not measured by economic success. Years ago, Alexander Solzhenitsyn wrote from the misery of the Soviet gulag that the object of life is not, as we have been led to believe, material prosperity but "the maturing of the soul."

But the good news is that we don't have to go to a Siberian prison camp to understand what Solzhenitsyn was talking about. In fact, I think that many people have seen in the excesses of the 1980s and in the soaring stock market gains of the late 1990s that material prosperity alone cannot satisfy.

Author Tom Wolfe made that point very clearly in his most recent book. Wolfe has long been a sharp social critic of American culture. His novel *The Bonfire of the Vanities* skewered Wall Street's "greed is good" mentality of the 1980s.

Wolfe took eleven years to write his next book, *A Man in Full,* which takes on the lives, prejudices, and politics of the super rich in Atlanta. By the book's end Wolfe's protagonist, a real estate developer named Charlie Croker, has abandoned his lifelong pursuit of wealth.

In an unforgettable press-conference scene, Croker talks

about people's search for satisfaction through travel, estates, expensive diversions, and acquisitions. "What is it you're looking for in the endless quest?" he asks. "Tranquillity. You think if only you can acquire *enough* worldly goods, *enough* recognition, *enough* eminence, you will be free, there'll be nothing more to worry about, and instead you become a bigger and bigger slave."[1]

I agree. Wealth sought for its own sake can never satisfy. In the end it always enslaves.

But if we see money as a *tool*, not an end in itself, it can be used for great good.

Over the years as I've reflected on what Glennis and I have learned about success and its benefits for others, I've hesitated to write a book. As you know from my story, I'm an action person, not a word person!

But as time has gone by, I've felt an obligation to share. We've learned a lot. I've profited from hard knocks, mistakes, experiments, and relationships with others—all through the grace of God. And I've learned how to work hard with excellence.

Most important, I believe that the principles I've learned about success can be shared—not just at the level of what it takes to succeed in business, though that may well come. But I mean *real* success: faithfulness to the deep, unchanging principles that carry us through life with fulfillment, bearing good fruit in our own lives and in the experiences of all those we touch.

That kind of success is buoyant, like helium. As we rise, it inevitably lifts others. It is available for all who seek it.

[1] Tom Wolfe, *A Man in Full* (New York: Farrar, Straus, and Giroux, 1998), 722.

And often, it comes hand in hand with financial rewards—
although I can't guarantee that if you apply the principles
you'll end up with a $25 million business deal at dinner one
night!

But I *can* guarantee that you'll experience *real* success, the
accumulation of life's true treasures. Again, those treasures
are found not in the wallet but in the soul. They are rooted in
the most essential relationships we enjoy as human beings:
our bond to God, to our families, and to the friends and colleagues around us, whatever season of life we're in.

These principles apply to any person running a small business, any franchiser or franchise owner, any manager in a corporate environment, and, in fact, anyone running a household
these days, which in many cases is very similar to running a
small corporation!

They also apply to students, coaches, retirees, the newly
married, whomever. Although I have distilled them from my
Merry Maids experiences, they can apply to men and women
in *any* type of business, in *any* season of our shared human
journey.

Because of that, I call them the seven principles of *real*
success—not just in business, but in life itself!

Part Two
The Seven Principles of Real Success

CHAPTER 13

Principle One

PUT PEOPLE FIRST:
Serve Those You Lead by
Building Them Up

The first principle of real success is the most essential.
All the others build on it. I've seen its power in corporate
boardrooms, political campaigns, in the franchise industry,
and around the hometown breakfast tables at the Hillcrest
Restaurant. It applies everywhere.

And I first used it as a principle when I had the opportunity to work with a woman I'll call Betty.

The Betty Principle

It was 1967, and I had just taken over management of the largest snack-food plant in the world. My predecessor in the job
hadn't done very well managing the five hundred people who
worked there. There had been several union walkouts on his
watch, and profits were way down.

I was thirty years old and hadn't managed this kind of situation before. I didn't quite know what to expect. But I did know I wanted to turn that plant around.

On my first day I was walking around the production floor, trying to get a feel for the place. An older woman with a worn face and a furrowed brow planted herself in front of me.

"Good morning!" I said, smiling. "How are you? I'm Dallen Peterson. I'm your new plant manager."

"Humph," she responded, looking me over. She seemed less than impressed. "I just hope you're not a son of a [gun] like the last manager!"

I wasn't sure just what kind of response this warranted, so I just sputtered the first thing that came to mind: "Well, ma'am, I sure hope I'm not too!"

Later I consulted with the production manager. "Who's that woman scowling over there on the chip line?" I asked.

"Oh," he said, "that's Betty. She's been here forever. Don't cross her. She's the union steward."

The next morning I strode onto the plant floor and headed straight toward Betty.

"Betty!" I said, putting my hand on her shoulder. "How are you doing today?"

"Humph!" she responded.

Every day when I came to work, I would walk the floor, and I made a point to walk over to Betty, put my hand on her shoulder, and greet her by name. I would tell her that she was doing a great job and that I appreciated her hard work.

Pretty soon Betty would wave when she'd see me coming. Then she actually grinned at me. Before long she was telling me all about everything that was going wrong at the factory.

Within a year, that failing plant had become the most profitable at Fairmont Foods. And when I left that position two years later, Betty actually cried at my farewell party. She had become one of my most loyal colleagues at that plant.

Why?

Because every day I took the time to walk where she walked. I reached out to touch her. I called her by name. I encouraged her. And I treated her with courtesy.

The elements that I applied in my relationship with Betty more than thirty years ago are very basic. But they are also the foundation of real success in any human enterprise. *You must put people first.* If you affirm people and build authentic relationships based on integrity, trust, and respect, they will follow you—and so will success.

A PAIR OF HANDS?

Your ability to apply the Betty Principle will depend on your basic view of human beings.

Some executives see people as secondary both to production and to advancing their own careers. They're willing to put people second, perhaps. But not first.

You've probably heard Henry Ford's quote, "Why is it that I always get the whole person, when all I really want is a pair of hands?" It seems that Ford was more concerned with cars than colleagues; he would have reveled in today's digitized assembly systems and computerized robot arms that have replaced many of the "whole" people who used to build his cars.

But the fact is, *people* are the beginning and end of the workplace. Even the toughest tycoon cannot lose sight of the adaptability, creativity, and brimming potential of the human beings who produce his or her product or service. The workplace is not a pristine, emotionless utopia of production and profit. Such a place does not exist. And if it did, it wouldn't be worth visiting.

THE WHOLE PERSON

So we can't just look at people as a pair of hands, the means toward the end of production. People are not machines.

The Betty Principle assumes, at root, that people are whole beings made in the image of God. And, as C. S. Lewis says,

> Christianity asserts that every individual human being is going to live for ever, and this must be either true or false. Now there are a good many things which would not be worth bothering about if I were going to live only seventy years, but which I had better bother about very seriously if I am going to live for ever. . . . If individuals live only seventy years, then a state, or a nation, or a civilisation, which may last for a thousand years, is more important than an individual. But if Christianity is true, then the individual is not only more important but incomparably more important, for he is everlasting, and the life of a state or a civilisation, compared with his, is only a moment.[2]

Simply put, to me that means there are no ordinary men and women. Each of us is unique among the six billion people on the planet. And we each house a soul that will live

[2] C. S. Lewis, *Mere Christianity* (New York: Macmillan, 1972), 73.

forever. This means that our colleagues, staff, acquaintances, friends, family, and customers will outlast the Dow Jones, the Internal Revenue Service, and the current presidential administration—not to mention our nation and the universe as we know it.

That's an overwhelming truth. Because of it, I believe that human beings, the *whole* people we lead and serve, must be our priority. Whether we're in the home, on the job, in a ministry or volunteer organization, *whatever* our field of endeavor, we must *put people first*.

Now, most people say they put people first; certainly no one advocates putting people last. But in the daily reality of the workplace, many executives end up putting profits first. Similarly, many parents affirm in theory that their children are more important than their careers but constantly demonstrate in reality that their jobs, in fact, come first. In practice many spouses put material concerns ahead of the people they say they love most.

But relationships are truly the most important priority. And I have found over the years that if you invest time in those you love at home and in those you serve at work, your family and your business will be strengthened immeasurably from the inside out.

NATURAL INCLINATIONS

I've always been a person who valued relationships. Perhaps it came from being an identical twin: right from conception, I was inextricably bonded to another person!

And then as I grew up on the farm with eight brothers and sisters, a close-knit community, and the ties of common religious faith, all these reinforced my inborn tendency to link with and look out for others. It may sound like Will Rogers' cliché, but in reality, I've never met a person I didn't like. Even Betty!

SUPERNATURAL INCLINATIONS

After my faith took a more personal turn in 1970, the Bible reinforced my natural tendency to focus on others. I saw how Old Testament Jewish law affirmed human dignity and justice for the oppressed and distressed; I saw how Christ treated *everyone* with compassion and respect, regardless of their economic or social status. (In fact, the only people he spoke to severely were the religious hypocrites of his day!)

Because of Christ's example, I tried to see my role in life as serving others—and that extended beyond my family and friends, beyond my natural comfort zones. As I've recounted earlier in this book, I tried to go out of my way to develop relationships with people who weren't just like me, people I never would have encountered if I just stuck with my clubs, my church, my neighborhood. Glennis and I opened our home to people who were homeless. We visited prisoners. We helped ex-offenders in any way we could. And as we became friends with those our society rejects, *we* were the ones who were abundantly blessed.

Over the years I have seen how people who are in "low" positions in our culture today—prison inmates, poor teenagers, service workers, factory workers—have a very keen discernment about the rest of us. Because they have often been mistreated by their superiors, they can tell very quickly if you're sincere or not. If you use people, they are the first to know it. Their openness to your message or leadership, their respect, and their loyalty to you will depend on whether, down deep, you really respect them.

WHAT ABOUT PEOPLE AND PROFIT?

In today's competitive environment, many businesspeople believe that putting people first is a nice idea but that it is incompatible with business profitability.

My friend Bill Pollard addresses this issue very well in his book, *The Soul of the Firm.*

Bill says, "At ServiceMaster, the task before us is to train and motivate people to serve so that they will do a more effective job, be more productive in their work, and yes, even be better people. It is more than a job or a means to earn a living. It is, in fact, our mission. Does this mean we are soft on profits?"

No. As Bill points out—citing ServiceMaster's incredible growth over the years—if you value people, the profits will come.

People *and* profit are part of our mission. Profit is how our owners measure us. It provides the resources to grow and develop people.

But profit for us is a means to a goal, not an end goal. . . . The accumulation of profits in the hands of a few is never justified. Marion Wade, our founder, used to remind us, "Money is like manure. It doesn't smell any better the more you pile it up." If we focused exclusively on profit, we would be a firm that had failed to nurture its soul.

Eventually, I believe, firms that do this experience a loss in the direction and purpose of their people, a loss in customers, and then a loss in profits.[3]

As I mentioned earlier, one reason ServiceMaster and Merry Maids have such a happy marriage is because of the similarity in corporate objectives and mission. Both companies have been very successful financially, but our profits have been a *means* toward the end of serving people and developing our employees.

If you treat people with respect and dignity, they will reflect that same respect to others. Our basic attitude toward others will ripple out from us to and through our families, office colleagues, teammates, and peers. In all of this we have the opportunity to create a wave of healthy attitudes that lifts others—or a tide of negative attitudes that sinks them.

Merry Maids' Corporate Culture

Every organization reflects the personality of its leader, for good or ill. Families are shaped by the character of the parents. Sports teams reflect their coach. If you go into any office on Capitol Hill, you can tell a lot about the representative or senator by the characteristics of the people who work for him or her: the workers mirror the boss. The atmosphere in Bill Gates's company headquarters is very different from that of Ted Turner's, which in turn is different from Service-Master's.

So it isn't surprising that from the start Merry Maids had

[3] C. William Pollard, *The Soul of the Firm* (New York: HarperCollins; Grand Rapids: Zondervan, 1995), 18–19.

a strong relational focus. For better or for worse, that's how God made me. And fortunately, it turned out for the better for Merry Maids because the priority of friendships, merged lives, and shared experiences forged bonds that both strengthened and superseded the company.

Who Are Your People?

At Merry Maids, I had four groups of people to consider. I treated each group with the same high degree of respect.

- *Our home-office staff.* These were the colleagues I saw on a day-to-day basis. They were a tight-knit, lean team made up of people who really enjoyed the challenge of building Merry Maids by attracting people with a similar mind-set, namely:

- *Franchise owners.* We were in the business of sales, of course. We not only had to keep our current franchise owners happy but also attract others to join us.

- *Team members.* Although our home office had little contact with the people who were employed by our franchises, we created the atmosphere that those individual team members breathed.

- *Customers.* Again, except for the early days when I was cleaning houses, doing estimates, and building the business, I didn't have much contact with individual customers. But great service meant serving our customers with detail-oriented, creative excellence. Our team members could do that with verve and confidence only if they felt supported and affirmed as workers.

Sometimes it's helpful to jot down a list of the various groups that look to you for leadership. If you're in business, that's pretty obvious. But we all need to remember our leadership responsibilities to those outside the business venue—to your children, students, volunteers you coordinate, and the Little League team you coach. Compile a list of those you lead, and determine creative, practical ways that you can put *them* first—not their report card, their score, their sales record, their numbers. If you build your relationships with those you lead, they will in turn be motivated to achieve.

From the beginning I tried to create a corporate environment that reinforced the value and priority of people. From day one, I practiced the Betty Principle of affirming each person however I could. As I learned from Betty, the first element of that principle is spending time with people. That means walking where they walk.

WALK

"Management by walking around"—MBWA—is taught in any good business school as part of its management curriculum. But it's astounding to me how few executives actually practice this potentially powerful principle.

Many business leaders start with great relationships with their colleagues. When the company is small and everyone is pulling together, the camaraderie is usually quite strong.

As the business grows, too many company presidents and CEOs unintentionally begin to wall themselves off. Preoccupied with the bottom line or investors or any of the perks and new problems that come with success, they isolate themselves behind a protecting phalanx of secretaries, assistants, and officers.

There, instead of being more efficient, I think they become more removed from reality, dependent on glossily packaged reports as to how the business is going and on sanitized memos from their Human Resources department as to how employees are faring.

But the rarified atmosphere of the corporate wing doesn't allow you to get a good whiff of the real morale of your company. And if people never see their leader except from a distance, they assume that he or she does not care about them.

Some time ago, while visiting a corporate headquarters, I spent some time with some staff people I knew on the second floor. When the company president heard I was in the building, he hurried down from his executive suite and arrived in the staff offices to greet and welcome me. (I own a lot of stock in this company.)

After he left, the staff people told me they had been amazed to see him on their floor. "We've been in this building for a year and a half," they said, "and that's the first time he's come down to our area."

Some executives seem to think that leadership requires some sort of lofty mystique and removal from the day-to-day operations of those who are in the trenches.

I think that mystique is a terrible mistake. It's a signal— unintended, I'm sure—that the leader doesn't care, can't relate, and can't be bothered. And people don't readily follow a leader who sends those signals. People may perform their tasks and may respect the boss with some degree of awe or fear, but they won't have the deep-seated loyalty, creativity, and commitment that comes with knowing and loving their leader.

SPEND TIME IN THE TRENCHES

During World War II, when Dwight D. Eisenhower was the supreme commander of the Allied Forces in Europe, he didn't *have* to visit the U.S. troops. He had generals and colonels and majors and lieutenants and sergeants—layers and layers of people "underneath" him—who could carry his message to the men in the trenches.

But General Eisenhower went to the soldiers. In the weeks before D day, he visited twenty-six divisions, twenty-four air-fields, five ships of war, and countless depots, shops, hospitals, and other installations. He believed that the troops—young men in their late teens and early twenties—should see the face of the man who was sending them into battle. Ike would shake their hands and ask them about their hometowns. He'd put his arm around their shoulders and talk about cattle ranching in Texas or dairy farming in Wisconsin.

In this one-on-one contact, General Eisenhower wasn't forgetting his exalted role; he didn't become less authoritative to the troops because he took the time to come to them.

Quite the contrary. These young men who were about to fight for their lives to defeat the Nazis did so with more confidence and commitment because they knew that their supreme commander cared about them, that he was a real person who could relate to them and their concerns.[4]

In the business world, our mission is not the life-and-death mission that the troops of World War II faced. But the

---

[4] See Stephen E. Ambrose's great book *The Victors: Eisenhower and His Boys: The Men of World War II* (New York: Simon and Schuster, 1998).

dynamic is the same: Human nature demands that real leaders *connect with their followers* and walk where they walk.

As a Christian, I can't help but point out that Jesus Christ demonstrates the divine example of this kind of leadership. Christianity purports that God himself became a man so that he would experience everything that we experience. He became like us so that we can one day become like him.

So, following his example, the essence of leadership requires that I spend real time among the people I lead so that I can know their real needs. And that's not just a perfunctory jog through the office now and then.

OPEN DOORS

In the service industry your employees are your only major assets. At Merry Maids, beyond a few vacuums, spray bottles, and uniforms, we didn't have a product. In the home office our only reason for being was to serve franchise owners.

So I tried to create an environment that was very people oriented. Although our executive wing was professionally presented so we could create a good impression for potential franchise owners—and we all dressed in very professional attire—we cultivated an informal environment. My door was always open unless I was having a private meeting. I would come in early in the mornings, and often Jim, a warehouse worker in the resource center, would stop by and have a cup of coffee with me.

And often at the end of the Merry Maids workday, I would put drinks and snacks out on the table in my office. People got in the habit of stopping by to talk and unwind. That, too, kept me in touch.

But the main opportunity to literally touch people was when I would walk the halls of the office every morning. I had no agenda. I would just greet people, see how they were doing, put my arm around their shoulders.

As I walked, I learned a lot. I might stroll through the resource center and see someone with a frustrated look on his face. "How's it going?" I'd ask.

Invariably, people would respond, "Oh, fine," even if the roof was caving in on top of them. But if I pressed just a bit further with a second question, they would usually open up.

"Well, our computer system was down yesterday afternoon, and now I'm really behind in getting these orders out." Or whatever.

Through conversations like that, I could personally encourage the person, learn something, help find a solution, and address the likelihood of similar problems in the future. Those were great payoffs in themselves. And the corresponding benefit of employee trust and loyalty could not be measured.

But if I was sitting in my office with the door shut, it's not likely that anyone would send me a memo about the problems he or she was confronting—until those problems escalated into some huge, unmanageable crisis.

And if I had stayed in my office, I might never have developed a real relationship with our controller, Carla. Carla was superbly gifted as a number cruncher, but she was fairly shy. I saw that she was extremely nervous and uneasy if she ever had to come to my office to deliver a report or give me a briefing.

So I made a habit of going to Carla on my rounds each morning. As a result, I was up-to-date on all our franchise numbers, and Carla was comfortable, productive, and extremely loyal because she knew I cared enough to come to *her*.

In short, executives who think that investing face time with their people is a waste of time are missing premium insights that they can gain no other way.

So first thing every morning, I would touch forty people personally. That human connection was one of the chief elements of Merry Maids' success.

GET ON YOUR KNEES

As our company grew, I would also make sure that at least twice a year I would appear at some franchise and go out and clean houses with a crew. I would wear the uniform and the knee pads, and the team members wouldn't know that I was coming.

Once they got over their shock that the president of the company was on his hands and knees, scrubbing the kitchen floor while they vacuumed the family room, they—and their franchise owners—thought it was the best thing they'd ever seen. (I would also be sure to attend the morning teammate meetings whenever I visited franchises so that I could interact with the workers, not just the owners.)

Now you won't find a whole lot of success books that advocate that you hit the floor on your knees. And of course, you may not have the opportunity to do that literally, as I did.

But the principle here is priceless. It applies in every field of human endeavor. *We must serve those we lead.*

Success is not about clawing your way to the top and lording it over those beneath you. Real success is about building relationships with those you lead, showing them you care for them, and showing them that you understand what they are experiencing. It's about helping them rise to whatever level of success they can achieve and then giving them the credit. Real leaders don't need fancy titles and imposing offices to show their authority. They have enough confidence to kneel among their people.

ENCOURAGE

Encouragement by example—like wearing those knee pads—is incredibly important. I've found that senior executives tend to be highly motivated and inner-driven. Sometimes we can forget that the troops aren't necessarily as driven as we are. They need positive feedback!

As any parent, teacher, or coach can tell you, people are motivated to succeed further when you focus on what they are doing well. When I first applied the Betty Principle thirty years ago, I affirmed the great job she was doing. And as I did so, I found that her negative, sour attitudes began to evaporate.

It's fun to find creative, tangible ways to express appreciation. Like many companies, Merry Maids always gave bonuses at the end of the year. We took care to design excellent retirement packages and 401(k) plans, and the like. But we also tried to recognize people's hard work in tangible ways that they could enjoy right away.

For example, our yearly seminar was a great time of celebration and fellowship for our franchise owners. But it was also a boatload of stress for our home-office staff. They would work like dogs for weeks beforehand and sometimes slept very little during the seminar itself.

So after the seminar was over, we would throw a big banquet for the home staff to express appreciation for their labors.
I would always make sure that the banquet was more elegant
and sumptuous than the banquets for our franchise owners
during the seminar. And, believe me, the home-office staff
noticed.

And, of course, we would always honor people's birthdays,
graduations, or other milestones. Balloons, flowers, and cakes
may seem mundane, but they are physical expressions of spiritual values. They *show* people what they need to know most:
"We care about you. *You* are important."

Sometimes companies *tell* people such things on annual
reviews and such, and that's great. It's important to have that
information in the file. But *telling is never as strong as showing.*
We tried to *demonstrate* our commitment and appreciation to
people, not just articulate it to them every once in a while.

The best ways to affirm people are often the simplest. As
I walked through the offices each day, I would know who was
doing an especially good job. Spontaneous, generous praise,
particularly in front of others, is one of the most powerful
tools any executive, manager, mother, coach, or teacher can
use to build confidence and loyalty with those we lead. People
are more motivated by public recognition than they are by
bonuses and pay hikes.

Praise should be specific, sincere, and never mixed with
criticism. It seems to be human nature, whether in a marriage, a family, or a company, to follow a compliment with
a critique: "You've done so well with *x,* if you'd only just
work on *y* . . ."

I would follow up verbal kudos with handwritten notes,

particularly to our franchise owners. I would keep a stack of note cards with stamped envelopes, and if I was on an airplane or waiting for an appointment, I would jot personal notes to people who were making a difference.

We also created certificates of achievement and appreciation. We featured top performers in our company newsletter and gave awards at our annual seminars. We created levels of achievement so that new franchise owners who had just met their first major goal felt a sense of accomplishment and recognition. And as they saw their colleagues from franchises across the country receive awards for the next level up, and the next, and the next, all the way to the company's premiere honor, they had a clear vision of the fact that escalating success was truly achievable.

Whether you're raising a family or building a company, praise is an extremely basic concept. Yet many people in leadership forget to give it. Many managers give feedback only when it's negative, only when things aren't going well, or when they're getting pressure from their superiors.

That type of negative communication creates a downward spiral in performance, confidence, and relationships. And it's highly contagious. I've seen situations in which a single leader's negative attitude has infected the whole corporation.

Certainly criticism is sometimes necessary, but it must be given in an affirming way that values the *person* and seeks simply to help refine the *behavior*. It must be clear that your end goal is to *serve* the person by encouraging—maybe even pushing—him or her to grow.

Sometimes people think they've grown all they can. They

lack confidence about their innate abilities. When that's the case, the most loving thing to do is to push them—even when *they* feel that you're nudging them right over the edge of the cliff.

PUSH

For example, Greg Hase was just twenty-one years old when he started with us at the Merry Maids home office in Omaha. Today Greg and his wife, Laurie, own a very successful Merry Maids franchise in Sioux City, Iowa. But back in 1984, Greg was very nervous the day we promoted him from a warehouse worker to the manager of our resource center.

He still lacked confidence when it came to presenting himself in public, so I decided that it would be good for Greg to make a presentation during our annual seminar in Omaha that fall.

"No way," Greg told me. "I've never spoken in front of a crowd before. Can't do it."

"You're the resource center manager now," I said, "and I want you to make a presentation of some of our new products."

"I can't do it," Greg said unequivocally.

"Yes, you can," I said just as firmly.

"I'll be too nerv—" he started, but then I broke in.

"You have to. It goes with the job."

I worked with Greg on the side, coaching him and affirming him in the fact that *he knew what he knew*—and other people didn't. He could be confident, and he could help them by telling them about his job.

The big day came, and several hundred people packed the

auditorium in the Red Lion Inn where we held our seminars at that time. When his part in the program arrived, Greg hesitantly walked toward the podium, squinting in the bright spotlights, his face sweaty.

Clutching his script, Greg leaned toward the microphone and cleared his throat.

"Uh . . . ," said Greg.

The crowd waited expectantly for his report.

"W-well," he stammered, "if this darn podium would just stop shaking, maybe I could read my notes!"

People burst into laughter and applause, and from that day forward, Greg was a natural in front of a microphone. He became one of Merry Maids' biggest hams. Today we can't get him to shut up!

RESPECT

Happily, the majority of the Merry Maids franchises we sold came through the referrals of other franchise owners. Franchise owners have typically been excited enough about Merry Maids and its potential to spread the news to their friends. It wasn't just because of the financial rewards. Lots of people earn money at jobs they dislike and wouldn't wish them on anyone else. But we treated our franchise owners with respect and encouragement, and they wanted to pass that experience on to their friends and family.

I did four extremely simple things to foster that sense of respect, right from the moment I met someone.

First, be on time for appointments. That's so basic it seems laughable—except for the fact that some executives seem to pride themselves on being late. They take outside calls during meetings with others, come late, and leave early, rushing about to show how busy and important they are. But that behavior communicates only a sense of boorish disrespect for the person kept waiting.

Certainly emergencies arise, but they are the exception. The well-disciplined executive is prompt and focused solely on the person in front of him or her.

One new franchise owner told me that he had joined Merry Maids—rather than a rival company he was considering—because he could always set his watch by me. I called him exactly when I said I would. I respected his time.

Second, do what you say. Enough said.

Third, finish what you start. Ditto.

Fourth, always say "please" and "thank you." We all learned such basics when we were toddlers, but I'm astonished by how many men and women in management seem to think that good manners are no longer a necessity. (Some of that comes from the offensive notion that discourtesy, like lateness, indicates power.)

My friend Carlos Cantu, retired president and CEO of ServiceMaster, has impeccable manners. Carlos once asked management guru Peter Drucker how he would define people skills in the workplace.

Dr. Drucker looked up and said simply, "Two words."

"Yes?" asked Carlos.

"Good manners," replied Drucker.

Courtesy costs nothing. It comes from the attitude of the heart. If managers are imperious, arrogant, and disrespectful of their employees, the first things they'll drop are "please," "thank you," and "excuse me"—the nuts and bolts of respect for others and the most basic elements of a healthy work environment.

When I think of courtesy and respect in the workplace, I think of Dot and Jack Hynes.

The People Business

After almost fifty years of marriage, Dot and Jack Hynes still act like the high school sweethearts they once were. The vitality of their relationship is the strength of their Merry Maids franchise, the largest in the United States. To me, Dot and Jack embody what Merry Maids is all about: building people up and helping them to grow.

Dot and Jack's Merry Maids story began just about where Glennis's and mine did. Jack was an engineer with the Pfizer Corporation, responsible for managing the entire start-up operations of new plants. It was an intense job with a lot of travel: Dot, weeping, would drive Jack to the airport on Monday mornings, and he would get back into town on Friday evenings.

"I wish we could spend more time together," Dot would sob.

By 1980, with their children grown and out of the home, Dot cast about for something to occupy her time. Seeing the growing number of women in the workplace, she at first thought about starting her own maid-service company. Fortunately for me, she didn't!

Instead, Dot joined Pfizer, working as Jack's office manager. She stashed her paychecks into a nest egg for five years.

Then, in 1985, having heard about Merry Maids through friends, Dot and Jack visited Omaha to learn more about the company, and they spent two days grilling Dale and me.

"Why do I need you?" Dot asked bluntly. "I could just start my own business."

"You could," I agreed. "But we could save you a lot of time and trouble. We've already made the mistakes and gotten the bugs out of our systems. Why reinvent the wheel? Why not hit the ground running?"

Eventually they agreed, and Dot took her nest egg and spent $12,500 to buy a Merry Maids franchise in Howard County, Maryland, one of our first on the East Coast. Jack told her that if she got the business up and running well, he would take early retirement from Pfizer and join her at Merry Maids.

Jack almost changed his mind, though, when he came to Omaha for training. We took the two of them out to be part of a housecleaning team. Jack had been a very pampered husband, and Dot stared in amazement at the unprecedented sight of Jack down on his hands and knees, diligently scrubbing someone's kitchen floor.

"If you do a good job on a house," I told them, "the customer will tell four people about you. But if you do a bad job, the customer will tell eleven people about how terrible Merry Maids is. The work has to be done right."

Dot and their daughter Debbie opened their Merry Maids office on March 1, 1986. They sat in their little rental space and stared at each other.

"Which comes first," asked Dot, "the chicken or the egg? Customers or maids?"

I had told Dot during training that if she went by the book—the Merry Maids operations manual—she would be successful. Dot is a very thorough and meticulous person. She went by the book.

Dot and Debbie used doorhangers, they consulted with other successful franchise owners, they hired their first maids . . . and within seven months, they were grossing $8,000 a week. In October 1986 they were voted Rookies of the Year at our annual seminar in Omaha. The following April, Jack kept his word, took early retirement, and joined Dot in the business. Today their franchise—with eighty employees in three offices— grosses well over $2 million a year. They were the first Merry Maids franchise to break $50,000, then $60,000 (and who knows how much by the time you read this) a week in sales.

That's an impressive business, particularly when you consider the fact that Dot and Jack don't put their customers first. Of course they provide excellent services, and their customers are very happy, but the Hyneses' first priority is their *employees.*

"A lot of our ladies are single mothers or have been through difficult times in their lives," Dot says. "Some of them don't have much confidence when they first come to us. We try to build them up, increase their self-respect. If they feel good about themselves and their work, then they'll do a great job for the customer."

Dot doesn't call her employees "maids." She feels that referring to them as "ladies" or "teammates" has a stronger sense of dignity.

Marie is a good example of the kind of people who work with Dot and Jack. When Marie started working for them in 1987, she was a single mom with five kids. She had no car, no driver's license, and had never owned a home. During her interview with Dot, she couldn't look Dot in the eyes. "She had no self-esteem," Dot says.

But Marie started working with Merry Maids, and gradually she began to thaw. She saved some money. With Dot's encouragement, she studied for her driver's test and got her license. The Hyneses helped her get her first car, a blue Geo Metro, and Jack helped her figure out what was under the hood. And on her tenth anniversary with the Hyneses, they surprised her with flowers, balloons, and a big cash bonus.

You can boil it all down to one main principle: Love. "Our family has grown up and gone," Dot says. "The ladies are our family. Many of them don't even get a hug at home, but when they come into our office, they get hugs, a listening ear. Some of them have told me things that they've never told their own mothers."

Like many Merry Maids owners, the Hyneses have made the business a family affair. Their daughter Debbie now has her own office, their daughter Darlene and her husband bought a franchise, and Jack's brother and nephew have both owned franchises.

"We'll never retire," says Jack. "Why would we? We travel or take time off whenever we need to. We're together, and we're working with people we care about. And besides all that, we're having fun!"

Dot and Jack were Merry Maids regional coordinators for more than a decade. They would pass on their sense of fun to prospective franchise owners—and they were also very clear about Merry Maids' philosophy of putting people first.

"You're going to derive your income from the cleaning business," Jack would tell new franchise owners. "But you're in the *people business*. If you can't deal with people with empathy and respect, you may as well get out."

Dot and Jack illustrate it beautifully: Respect of one's

fellows enhances people's innate ability to succeed. Respect builds a strong and cohesive workplace. It also leads naturally into Merry Maids' corporate objective to *help people develop.*

REFLECT

Sometimes the best way to help others grow is to gently help them see what they could do better.

We all need help with this, even though it's painful. After all, most of us have twenty-twenty vision or better when it comes to seeing *other* people's behavior. But most of us are rather myopic when it comes to discerning what *we're* doing wrong.

Sometimes at Merry Maids we were able to push people onward to greater levels of success just by holding up a mirror to them—reflecting to them work behaviors that weren't quite up to snuff.

As we grew over the years, I was concerned about our corporate image. Keeping the Merry Maids identity and ethos consistent in the home office was one thing, but assuring consistency among hundreds of franchise owners across the country—and their thousands of employees—was very difficult.

For example, I wanted to make sure that the first impression that any Merry Maids office made on a potential customer was overwhelmingly positive. Ninety-nine percent of the time, that first impression comes when a potential client calls the local franchise office. If the phone is answered with professionalism and warmth, you're on your way. If that first phone impression is poor, then *they're* on *their* way—right down the street to your competitor.

Early on it became clear that a number of our franchise

owners weren't putting priority on telephone etiquette. So I hired our youngest daughter, Karma, to call all of our franchise offices, applying for a job as a maid. Karma made more than four hundred phone calls across the country, and we recorded them all.

At the next series of meetings in each region around the country, we let our franchise owners hear themselves or their assistants handling these calls. Many were embarrassed to hear how they sounded and agreed with us that their telephone manners needed an overhaul.

A month later one of our home-office staff members called one hundred offices in a similar test. The changes in telephone etiquette were remarkable.

We gave this reflective feedback in such a way that *we* weren't correcting our people. They had had no idea how they sounded. So they corrected *themselves*. Their response was the beginning of our corporate policy and how each franchise across the nation answers the telephone to this day: "It's a great day at Merry Maids!"

Putting people first involves helping them to see themselves more clearly so they can grow. You also have to figure out how to continue motivating them toward success.

BUILD MOMENTUM

What I've found over the years is that you can't really *say* things that motivate others. Sure, we all get inspired and excited when we hear a really great speaker, but often the inspiration evaporates before we have a chance to put the speaker's ideas into practice.

I think that lasting motivation comes when people feel

that they are part of something exciting and that they have something unique to contribute. You motivate people when you give them the opportunity to do things they could not do without you. Many of the staff people and owners I worked with at Merry Maids over the years were people with tremendous potential that had not yet been realized. We gave them the opportunity to succeed by providing them with the tools to do it and the model of what success could look like. Then we jumped in and did it with them!

That leads to the next principle of real success.

First you employ the Betty Principle: Put people first, and build *up* those who look to you for leadership.

Then you build them *together*. You create a cohesive, dynamic *community*.

Principle
Two

CREATE COMMUNITY:
Serve Those You Lead by
Building Them Together

When Bill Pollard and I were talking about this book, Bill shared one of his early lessons at ServiceMaster with me. He had been with the company about six months learning various aspects of the franchise business. Then one day he said to his boss, "I don't get it. Once our franchise owners have been trained and are up and running, why do they still pay us royalty fees?"

"You still don't understand the business, do you?" Bill's boss said. "They pay those fees because *they want to belong.*"

Bill's anecdote illustrates a key truth that is essential to real success in any endeavor. Whether you are leading a team, a family, a business, or a group of any kind, whether you're in charge of five people or five thousand, you must instill a sense of belonging. That means you must create a feeling of *community*.

From the beginning I never saw franchise sales or any other aspect of Merry Maids as merely a business. As I've said, I was interested primarily in *building relationships.* First, I built them with individuals. Then I tried to create a sense of community, building people together into a strong, working company. Every team, family, business, or organization runs according to these dynamics.

I understood that the franchise business is lonely for the franchise owners. I needed to build a sense of belonging so that individual owners would feel that they were part of a much bigger group, part of something strong and significant.

We tried to communicate this in every way we could. When Curt Holstein bought his Merry Maids franchise back in 1986, his son Ben was six years old. When Curt came to my brother Dale's office to sign his franchise agreement, Dale very solemnly brought Ben in for the proceedings. Dale had prepared a little contract for Ben to sign too. It included clauses like "I agree to help Mommy and Daddy with their new business." While Ben's contract wasn't exactly legally binding, it served a far more important purpose. It bound the Holsteins into the Merry Maids community with the strong sense that this was a *family* affair.

Some people may feel, well, it's just a housecleaning business. There's no glamour or power in that. Why the big deal about community?

But even the most mundane work, if it is done well, has intrinsic worth. It ennobles the worker. And when individual owners felt they were part of the powerful Merry Maids momentum thundering down the tracks, that sense of community created great corporate excitement, pride, and enthusiasm.

Building Your Team: Pass On the Vision

People feel that they belong to a community and invest in making it stronger if they understand the corporate vision and how they are contributing toward reaching the corporate goals. This works in families as well: every member needs to understand the family goal so that each person can have a clear expectation and understanding of his or her part in helping the family fulfill that goal.

When President Kennedy charged NASA with putting a man on the moon by the end of the 1960s, he gave them a clear, compelling goal. It captured the imagination of the space agency's staff at every level and in turn created a sense of corporate unity, purpose, and drive.

Merry Maids wasn't trying to put a man on the moon, but we followed the same principle. Everyone in the company knew our big-picture vision: to be number one, the biggest and best homecleaning service in the industry.

And along the way, everyone knew the more quantifiable immediate goals. I remember when we were all shooting to sell our one hundredth franchise. We all pulled together to reach that mark, whether through public relations, sales efforts, or franchise owners' simply succeeding and telling their friends. And when we sold that one hundredth franchise, *everyone* celebrated.

And then, of course, we all worked with a sense of shared passion and purpose toward the *next* goal.

It is the responsibility of the leader to serve his or her people by instilling that sense of passion and excitement. That doesn't come from memos or corporate pronouncements. It comes from people being in touch with the leader and seeing his or her own excitement, integrity, and commitment.

Joy Flora, Merry Maids' president, is a great example of this. Joy has considerable management and corporate experience through her work with ServiceMaster. She's also a former Merry Maids franchise owner, so she knows the day-in, day-out joys and trials of the business. She has a leader's sense of passion and excitement about the big picture, and staff and owners also know that she can identify with the small daily challenges they face.

Another key to building your team is to create unity in the midst of diversity.

Building Your Team: Create Unity in Diversity

I thought of Merry Maids as an extended family. And like any family, that meant that even though we all had the same name, we were all extremely different. I wasn't looking for clones.

So in spite of Merry Maids' Judeo-Christian religious foundations, we were, of course, open to people who came from different religious traditions—or none. We wanted people who were open to our objectives, people who had the heart and personality to grow, to help others grow, and to have a good time in the process. From the top down we wanted Merry Maids to have a sense of excitement, momentum, and passion for real success.

So there was a great camaraderie in the company, a great oneness of spirit and intention. But at the same time we enjoyed great diversity, bringing in people from a variety of ethnic backgrounds, traditions, and life experiences. We ran the gamut from dentists to carpenters, from farmers to teachers, from middle managers to homemakers. And to me, there was no greater pleasure than to look over the audience at one of our yearly seminar meetings and see faces representing hundreds of different backgrounds and experiences—and yet all united in our common vision and mission.

If you have only uniformity—people who all think the same way—your community weakens. You lose the strength that comes from contending points of view sharpening one another and eventually producing the best ideas or solutions.

And if you have only diversity, your strength is dissipated. You end up with a company that's not a community, just a conglomerate of dozens of splintered cliques that all want to head in their own directions.

So at Merry Maids we worked hard to understand the strengths, weaknesses, and diverse personalities of those we brought into the company so that we could build healthy unity among people who were different.

Building Your Team: Use Interviews As Inner Views

Sometimes executives become too far removed from the interview process. But particularly as one begins to build a business, there is no more important investment of time than bringing like-hearted people into your organization.

It's crucial to ask the right questions and to trust your own intuitions. Again, you aren't looking for clones of yourself—that would be dangerous—so you needn't look for people who have identical goals or backgrounds or experiences, even if at first blush you feel most comfortable with them.

What you're looking for is people of similar *spirit*. You don't want people who see their jobs as simply a series of tasks, workers who think they're just assembling a big pile of rocks. You want people who can share your vision and enthusiasm, people who realize that together, you're building a cathedral.

I always found the following questions helpful:

- Tell me about your most challenging—and least challenging—job.
- Tell me about the person you admire most and about a person you don't respect at all.
- Tell me about a time when something bad happened to you.
- Tell me about a time when you tried to help someone change.
- Tell me about a time when you had to overcome major obstacles to meet a job challenge.
- Tell me about a mistake you made in dealing with people.
- Tell me about the last time you made a major change.

A person's answers to these questions and the discussions that spin off from them can give you an excellent sense of his or her energy, scope, teachability, and discernment.

I found that weaker candidates focused on what had happened to them in the past—and not on why it happened. Stronger candidates would focus on what they learned and how those insights equipped them the next time they ran into a similar situation.

Weaker candidates didn't seem to have a cohesive, integrated philosophy by which they lived and learned. Stronger candidates were usually more discerning of their strengths, weaknesses, and limits. I respected that.

I looked first for people with positive, growth-oriented attitudes. Their experience, skills, and competence—though important, of course—were secondary.

Sometimes candidates can dazzle you with their experience, education, qualifications, and references. It's easy to want to hire someone because of his or her amazing résumé, even if he or she doesn't fit with your company ethos. We did it a time or two, but it's never worth it.

At the Merry Maids home office we didn't rely just on our own gut reactions to candidates. We also made sure that candidates were interviewed not only by managers but also by their peers, the people who would be working with them. That way our employees felt that they had a part in the decisions that affected them—a very important practice in a cohesive, community-oriented workplace.

In the same way that we listened carefully to candidates before we hired them, we tried to create a workplace atmosphere that fostered give-and-take between employees and franchise owners. There's nothing more important than excellent communication—and that doesn't happen automatically. You have to incorporate strong communication vehicles into your corporate community.

Building Your Team: Communicate Clearly

Whatever the institution—a marriage, a family, a business—communication is the first means by which a person puts his or her principles and beliefs into practice. I don't care how exalted a view you might hold intellectually about fellow human beings: what matters is how you treat them. Belief without corresponding actions means nothing.

We've all known political leaders or members of the clergy or CEOs who can make eloquent speeches about human dignity and then turn around and treat their support staff like dirt.

Well, at Merry Maids we didn't tolerate dirt. That meant that we had to live out our views about the priority of people every day in the workplace.

The first step, practically speaking, comes through communication: the clear, consistent exchange, both verbal and nonverbal, of ideas and information. And whether one is in a marriage, a family, or a business, communication must be mutual, not one-sided.

Clear and fruitful communication doesn't come naturally. We all live inside our own heads and assume that others know exactly what we're thinking or that they react to situations the way we do. But that's not the case. (Glennis would be the first person to tell you that no one else on the planet thinks the way I do.) So we have to take care to elicit information, ideas, and reactions from others. That takes work—because it means we have to *listen* more than we talk!

LISTEN

Usually people tell company executives or board members only what they think those people want to hear. When I was president of Merry Maids and would walk through the home offices, people habitually smiled brightly and told me that everything was great. They wouldn't open up unless I probed. When I traveled to far-flung franchises across the country, the same thing happened.

I would listen to people's comments and try to discern what they were *not* saying. I would ask follow-up questions that probed a bit deeper than the pat answer. On the road I would tell them, "I didn't travel fifteen hundred miles just to find out that everything's fine. I could have stayed home and saved some company money. What are your frustrations?"

And because of the integrity of our relationships, people would usually open up and tell me more. They would tell me about everything from shortages of teammates to moody office managers to quirky customers. It was helpful for them to be able to vent—and then I could help them come up with creative solutions. Excellent communication takes work: careful listening to what is said and not said, creative questioning, and a foundation of trust.

The main principle I employed in my communication with others is that I would never talk critically about any owner or staff member. Nothing would create distrust faster in my relationship with an owner. Sometimes I felt like a chaplain or a pastor with people: confidentiality was imperative. It was the basis for integrity and trust in our relationships.

We made sure that managers operated from the same mind-set. I encouraged them to sit down frequently with workers, either individually or in small teams, asking questions like What can the company do to make your job better? How can we create a better work experience for you? Then we would make sure, if at all possible, to put their suggestions into practice. If we couldn't, we would explain why. That way people knew we were really listening, and they also felt that they were an integral part of the company.

PRACTICAL COMMUNICATION TOOLS
Our most important internal communication tool was a very

simple one that grew naturally out of our very first day in business: the telephone log. Every officer and support-staff member (including me) logged the name and essential elements of the conversations they had with franchise owners and potential franchise buyers. At the end of the week everyone turned those logs over to me.

On Saturday mornings, when things were quiet, I would go into the office and review the logs. They became the source of my "to do" list for the following week. I would send congratulatory notes to owners who were hitting new sales levels, or I would send cards if I knew that someone's family member had been ill or that an owner was celebrating a birthday or anniversary. I would schedule a call with an owner who might be feeling disgruntled or discouraged.

In short, these phone logs allowed me to get a sense of how people were really feeling about the business and then to respond personally to their needs. I don't care how sophisticated or large a business or corporation might be; at the bottom line it is *relationships* that are most important. If people feel valued, if they feel that those in management really *care* about their lives and their concerns, then they feel confident. That confidence, in turn, brings success—both in terms of a strengthened relationship and increased energy for the work itself.

Once I had reviewed the phone logs, I had our receptionist post the calls by franchise owners. At the end of the month I would call or assign a staff member to call any owner who had not been contacted in the last thirty days.

We filed the phone logs by month and year. Should any owner complain about a lack of support from the home office, we could follow the paper trail to agree with or refute the claim.

We had several companywide publications. *Merry Maids
News,* a bimonthly newsletter for franchise owners, covered the
growth of the business, reported on owners' successes, and
informed readers of any new programs, incentive trips, and
general announcements. It conveyed a sense of excitement and
momentum; we wanted franchise owners to feel that they were
part of something large, something that was growing every week.

Maids Matter, now called *Team Talk,* was a quarterly publica-
tion for the team members themselves. We wanted them to feel
special and to have fun reading it. Our most popular feature was
the "customers say the darndest things" section. Franchise owners sent in the craziest and most complimentary communications from customers, and we never had any trouble filling that
page with comments such as: "Please do not let the dogs outside
at all. There are two baby birds out back, and they can't fly. If
the dogs get out, the birds will be dead, and the dogs will have
bird breath for a week!" (Bettendorf, Iowa). "We looked everywhere and couldn't find where Tipper the cat had hidden my
husband's hearing aid. But [the Merry Maids] found it!" (Afton,
Missouri). "My son's pet mice are loose! They are babies, and
they won't hurt you. Also, don't clean the bedroom to the left of
the bathroom. I let the guinea pigs out, and I can't catch them!"
(Joplin, Missouri). "Great job cleaning the house, but you did
not wash the Jeep or rake the leaves" (Princeton, West Virginia).
And, "Just work around Grandma. Her name is Gertrude, and
she is hard of hearing" (Prescott, Arizona).

Since our formal communication with owners was
bimonthly, we communicated with them weekly via computer
modem on the Merry Maids Bulletin Board. (Remember, this
was back in the mid-1980s. The on-line connections we take

for granted today were rather innovative back then.) Our on-line bulletin board contained news, operational tips, announcements, and case histories, all available for the owner's benefit at his or her convenience.

Another helpful communication tool was the quarterly franchise business analysis. Each owner closed out his or her weekly reports and submitted them to the home office each week. At the end of the quarter the home-office computer would document the last thirteen weeks' business figures and compare them to the figures for the previous year. Operations staff members would review these, looking for problems, trends, and improvements, and then call the owners to offer help or congratulations.

We also mailed random communications—announcements, flyers regarding new products, invitations to regional meetings, updates for operational manuals—to franchise owners about every ten days.

All of these tools were designed to let owners know that we were connected with them and thinking of them.

It was difficult, however, to generate communications *from* the field. We tried surveys and questionnaires in an effort to get owners' reactions and opinions, but responses were few and far between. So we ended up calling a representative sampling of individual owners to take our company's corporate temperature.

Building Your Team: Match Mentors

One of our most successful means of building community at Merry Maids was our buddy system, a kind of mentoring program throughout the company.

I know firsthand what a buddy can do for you. When I was in basic training in the army, I developed pneumonia during the sixth week of the eight-week stint. It was a cold February in Ft. Leonard Wood, Missouri, and I was as sick as a miserable dog. But I refused to go on sick call. I knew I would be hospitalized, and I had seen that once you fell behind in your training schedule, they'd put you in a later class. I was scheduled to get married on March 12, and I knew Glennis would kill me if I hadn't finished basic training and we had to reschedule our wedding!

My bunkmate, Joe, was a big, strapping guy. Joe carried my huge backpack as well as his own and helped me survive training maneuvers in the field. Joe is the reason I'm alive today because in the end, I completed basic training and got home in time to marry Glennis! Joe was the ultimate buddy.

At Merry Maids the buddy system was the basis of our "fast start" program, in which new franchise owners received intensive help to get to a $2,000-a-week gross sales within eight weeks.

In this program an experienced owner who had enjoyed good success would adopt a new owner in his or her region. It was considered an honor to be asked to be a buddy, and because of our practice of testing personality profiles, we had a good idea of which personalities would match well.

Of course, we weren't matchmaking for a lifetime, so we didn't try to engineer totally perfect alliances. But the system worked well: Once we had newcomers and old-timers linked, they would run with it. The mentor would walk the new person through every aspect of starting the business, from setting up the office to hiring that first maid, from the first cleaning to using our computer system.

We covered all of these aspects of the business in our home-office training program, of course, but it was interesting to see how the mentoring relationship really helped new owners hit the ground running and avoid some of the common pitfalls.

Buddies also called new owners at least once a week—and often once a day—and I saw how the friendships would grow, making the company stronger because of the strength of our corporate relationships with each other. New owners' motivation would be stronger as well, because they could visualize their own success as they were seeing it modeled in their mentors' success.

When the new owner reached the goal of that $2,000 weekly sales level, the mentor would then take on a new buddy. And many owners who had benefited from mentoring eventually became mentors for others.

The mentoring program was one of the most cost-effective ways to strengthen our company as a whole. First, it strengthened our ability to coach and comfort new owners. If a new franchise in Los Angeles was in trouble, we could not always jump on a plane and go there, but a local Merry Maids mentor in the region could help. It was a great way to multiply our ability to respond to needy new owners.

The mentors weren't paid for their services, although we paid any expenses they incurred. But the long-term satisfaction they derived and the long-term friendships they built were priceless. In addition, any time you coach someone else, you learn as much as he or she does.

That mentoring attitude pervaded our corporate community. Because our franchise owners' territories were exclusive to them, owners were not in competition with each other and were therefore eager to help one another. The more successful one franchise owner was, the better it was for his or her neighboring owner.

"Success begets success" was particularly true in our franchise system. Each owner's new and useful idea, each owner's success, raised the level of business acumen and swelled the tide for all the others.

Many of our Merry Maids franchise owners served as wonderful mentors for newer members of the team. Paul and Evy Hatjistilianos are just one example. Paul and Evy bought our first Merry Maids franchise on the East Coast, breaking into the Boston-area market in 1982. Their early days were tough: Paul remembers hiring his first maids on a Friday and then coming in the following Monday morning to find that they had quit over the weekend. So Paul and Evy changed from the business suits they had worn to do customer quotes, put on their cleaning clothes, and scrubbed houses all day.

Paul and Evy eventually built their business into a highly successful franchise. But even when they were comfortable and could have been out playing golf, they never forgot what it was like at the beginning. They served as regional coordinators several times during their nine years with Merry Maids and gave thousands of hours of mentoring encouragement to others along the way.

Paul and Evy held quarterly regional get-togethers. These BARF meetings (for Boston Area Regional Franchises!) brought together area franchise owners in a relaxed atmosphere with lots of food and drink to celebrate successes, talk about problems, and brainstorm solutions. Inevitably, when these BARF meetings ended, everyone left with renewed energy and a greater vision for success.

Paul also started offering daylong Saturday seminars for new owners. He would get together three or four new franchise owners and invite them to his office, where he would put together a teaching session on business basics. These owners had gone through Merry Maids training in Omaha, but now they were back home, in the thick of the battle, so to speak, and Paul felt he could offer hands-on encouragement and solutions that would help them achieve early success. I never even knew until years later that Paul was doing this—on his own time, when he could have been relaxing somewhere.

"I enjoy helping people," Paul says. "It was a lot of fun to help them succeed and to develop friendships along the way. It made our work more meaningful—because in the end, *people* are what it's all about."

Franchising is by definition a lonely enterprise. Individual owners often end up feeling that they are all alone, isolated from their colleagues and business community. That's why Paul and Evy's meetings, phone calls, and visits were so immensely helpful to those they mentored: they demonstrated to the new owners that they were part of a larger community, that they were connected to a whole, and that there were people who cared for them, understood their stresses, and could help them.

Building Your Team: Advocate Accountability

In the same way, Merry Maids today encourages accountability groups in which clusters of four or five franchise owners get together regularly to review their progress, discuss their problems, and spur one another on to greater sales levels. The groups also help members overcome their tendency toward complacency: owners hold one another accountable for goals they set at the last meeting! This peer pressure is a powerful tool to help build company community as well as to motivate individual owners to new heights of achievement.

Building Your Team: Have Fun

Back in our beginnings, our Merry Maids home office employed as summer interns a number of college students as well as new graduates of the University of Nebraska franchise study program. We encouraged college students to explore the challenges and potential of franchise businesses, and our interning program allowed us to mentor some incredible young people—like Rod Roberts, Jim Lovely, and Paul Hogan—who went on to become highly successful businessmen who now mentor others.

When we asked these students what was most important to them about their jobs, their priorities reflected the responses of a survey later done by the National Association of Colleges. They rated the following factors in order of importance:

- Enjoying what they do;
- Using their skills and abilities;
- Growing in personal development;
- Feeling that what they do matters;
- Receiving good benefits;
- Receiving recognition of good performance;
- Working with friendly colleagues;
- Working in a location they like;
- Receiving a generous salary;
- Working in team-oriented situations.

Older employees have more responsibilities and differ slightly in their priorities. But I found that regardless of people's ages, they ranked the growth-oriented factors as more important than issues of straight remuneration.

If you were to interview a random sample of Merry Maids franchise owners, you would see that same pattern. Many owners came to Merry Maids from the corporate world. Corporations are tremendous; I spent thirteen fruitful years working in one. But for people with a certain type of personality, they can be stifling. Before many franchise owners came to Merry Maids, they had begun to feel trapped in the layers of management bureaucracy, as I did. Heavy schedules of meetings, memos, and business travel were sapping their energy levels.

Of course, no organization or business is perfect because it is made up of flawed human beings. There will always be some degree of politics as long as human beings are involved. But we tried to design the Merry Maids environment so that we could feel free to focus on our work—and have fun with each other while we were doing it.

The key time for fun was during our annual seminars. These companywide meetings took place every fall, bringing owners from across the country together in Omaha. Our home-office staff knocked themselves out to put together a program that would equip and encourage the troops, from the most successful franchise owner to the person who had just joined the Merry Maids team the week before.

We brought in professional motivational speakers, conducted workshops on the practical concerns every franchise owner faced, and provided opportunities for everyone to interact with our management team.

We tried to show our owners as clearly as we could that they were important and that we really were a big family. We handed out awards to honor every conceivable achievement. We recognized team members who had contributed in outstanding ways to their offices' success.

We ate and laughed and talked informally in every setting imaginable, forging relationships that would give franchise owners the energy and momentum they would need to propel them forward to the next level of sales success.

At our seminars the "Merry Maids hug" became a corporate trademark. I know it sounds corny; hugging is not big in most business environments. But for us it came naturally, the most spontaneous way of connecting with another human being and saying, in effect, *"You* are important! We're with you! Way to go!"

The key thing we tried to build into the seminar experience was the element of surprise. People never knew what to expect—but they knew they would have fun.

One year Glennis and I greeted everyone at the hotel ballroom door wearing glittering rhinestone cowboy outfits with absolutely enormous white cowboy hats. Another year I dressed as a navy admiral with a gold braided jacket, hat, and pants. Given my height—or lack thereof—most people thought I looked like Napoleon.

We also cheerfully submitted ourselves to ridicule with truly atrocious lip-synching and dancing in Hollywood-style production numbers on stage. People loved to see us make fools of ourselves, and it reassured them that I was going to stick with the housecleaning business—because it was abundantly clear that I was not going to make it in show business.

One noteworthy production was the Maid Olympics. We brought six maid teams from across the country to Omaha to compete. They lit the Olympic flame in a toilet bowl with a scrub brush and then participated in such intensive sports contests as the vacuum cleaner obstacle course, the bucket sponge toss, the three-legged race (with their legs tied together with cleaning cloths). It was something less than sophisticated, but it made people laugh and drew them together.

We threw a lot of silly stuff into those seminars, but we also wanted our owners to feel pampered. We always made sure that things were first class, with sumptuous meals, fresh flowers, twinkling candles, and quality entertainment.

Our incentive trips were particularly lavish. We learned early on that going first-class normally costs only a bit more if you're a good negotiator. We took owners who were excelling to resorts like The Royal Hawaiian in Honolulu, the MGM Grand Hotel in Las Vegas, Las Brisas in Acapulco, the Hilton and Swan hotels in Walt Disney World, the Willard Inter-Continental Hotel in Washington, D.C., and on a Dolphin Cruise Line excursion. Owners never forgot those trips, which also continued to foster relationships.

Whatever the venue—a luxury cruise or a storefront office—laughter draws people together and strengthens relationships and the sense of corporate community.

That leads naturally to the next principle of success, which doesn't look *in* toward the team but *out* toward the customer.

Principle
Three

MASTER SERVICE:
Serve Your Customer
with Excellence

Merry Maids had been in business for about fourteen days,
and I was going out on my third sales call, trying to secure our
services for a very upscale home. The woman who lived there
was inquiring about our business; she had no idea it was just
two weeks old. I handed her my business card; she looked
down at it and then up at me again, taking note of my crisp
blue blazer and rich silk tie. "Mr. Peterson," she asked, "is your
company nationwide?"

I had just gotten those business cards that morning; they
were a nice, heavy stock and very professional. I was surprised
the ink was even dry, but they had communicated the impression I wanted to make, as had my choice of clothes: We were a
large, experienced company. Little did she know she was my
third customer!

"No, ma'am," I said. "But we will be one day!"

Excellence in Service

If you want to succeed in life, excellence in service is the third great principle. It runs the gamut from creating an excellent first impression—as I tried to do with that third Merry Maids customer—to creating an excellent final impression. That means doing what you say you'll do, on time, as perfectly as possible, with every extra beneficial detail you can think of.

When you achieve that goal in business, you needn't worry about your profits. They will come!

DON'T SHOW ME THE MONEY!

Ever since Cuba Gooding Jr. hollered, "Show me the money!" at Tom Cruise a few years ago in the hit movie *Jerry Maguire,* it's been a catchphrase. In the booming 1990s and the new millennium many businesspeople—and investors across the board—have been hollering the same thing. And the money has come rolling in.

I've enjoyed the crest of that wave as well. My investments have multiplied many times over in the strong economy of recent years, and for that I'm very grateful.

But I have to tell you, money has never been my bottom line. In fact, it's a big mistake to make it your primary goal. If you do, you'll lose not only your sense of priorities but your cutting edge of creativity. Success grows when you focus on *people,* not profits.

As I was developing Merry Maids' business concept, putting in all the hard work it took to get it running, and then going through its years of tremendous growth, I wasn't focusing on the money. I was focusing on our *service,* that we might shape Merry Maids into the best service company it could be.

LOTS OF MONEY, LITTLE TIME: GREAT OPPORTUNITY

Today the trends that originally paved the way for Merry
Maids and other service companies continue. Demographic
studies show that 70 percent of American women work outside the home. In 80 percent of all marriages, both spouses
work.

Those figures and the generally healthy economy mean
that service industries continue to have tremendous potential,
because even as people's discretionary *incomes* rise, their discretionary *time* tends to shrink. So for many folks in our target
market, time is actually more precious than money. They
want to spend it with their families or playing golf or getting
together with friends—*not* cleaning. So any domestic service
that can save time for people who have money is destined to
do well.

AT LEAST HE SHOWED UP!

The irony is that even though customers are more demanding
than ever, *poor* service has become a trend.

I ran into a neighbor the other day. She told me that she
had stayed home for hours that morning waiting for a repair-
man who had said he would be there promptly at 9:00 A.M.
At great inconvenience she had changed her plans in order to
let him in . . . and waited and waited until he finally arrived at
noon. I was struck by her conclusion: "Well, at least he showed
up!" It was as if that was the best she could expect.

Based on informal interviewing, I think the market is wide
open for companies that can get their act together and provide
plain old excellent, timely service. They could wipe out the
competition!

One example of this in the retail market is Nordstrom. The upscale department store arrived in a number of East Coast shopping malls some years ago, and customers were delighted by Nordstrom's "if you need it, we can do it" attitude. Their shoe department is legendary—if you have very large, very small, very narrow, or even different-sized feet, they will sell you the shoes you need. If you wander through their perfume and accessories departments you'll notice the lovely atmosphere. What's different? First, a tuxedoed pianist is playing a grand piano near the escalators. Second, they have personal shoppers to help you. Third, service is a definite priority. For one friend's trousseau, a Nordstrom manager showed up at her doorstep the day before the wedding with a last-minute alteration.

It's been interesting to see how Nordstrom's focus on service has not only drawn a loyal following for their stores but also upped the ante for other department stores. Since Nordstrom arrived in a mall outside Washington, D.C., for example, customers have noticed that their competitors, spurred on by Nordstrom's lead, are now providing markedly better customer service than they used to.

Elements of Superior Service

The principles of customer service are very basic. As Nordstrom illustrates, however, they become magic in the execution.

1. STAY CLOSE TO THE CUSTOMER

Many companies today are neglecting the most basic rule of all: Stay close to the customer. They're forgetting the fundamental truth that service is all about relationships with people. They're losing the human touch.

For example, I own a guest home in Florida. Like most Florida homes, it requires a lot of upkeep that I can't easily do myself. There's a lawn-care service, a tree service, a pool service, an extermination service, and a cleaning service—Merry Maids, of course!

With the exception of the last, I have yet to meet a single owner of any of those local companies. I might see a staff person come or go—and that's great—but I have no sense of *relationship* with an owner. So I don't have the same sense of loyalty or patience that I would have if the owner had cultivated me as a customer.

And God forbid that you do have a problem, because that's where it gets really sticky for a customer. The other day I was on the phone for fifty-two minutes (my phone automatically logs the length of calls) with a certain unnamed telephone company before I actually got hold of a live human being. An automated telephone-answering system is absolutely antithetical to good customer service. It is a convenience only for the company.

For the customer it is nothing but frustrating and infuriating because it is a very deliberate means by which companies remove themselves from actually having to deal with people. They forget that the customer is their very reason for being—and that attitude breaks every known law of good service.

At Merry Maids we had a cardinal rule that every franchise owner received a personal response from me, if needed, within twenty-four hours. Here's where technology came in handy as a tool: I could be in Japan or on an airplane or a boat or wherever, and I could get right in touch with the person. When today's technology facilitates old-fashioned communication, voice to voice, it's great. That type of connection is absolutely essential to cultivate customer relationships in today's impersonal, computer-driven society.

2. CULTIVATE COMPLAINTS

This is the second principle of great customer service. I don't mean you should do shoddy work so you'll get lots of complaints. I mean there is an art to *using* the complaints that will inevitably come to strengthen your service and in fact develop your customers. I found that if I responded to a dissatisfied client in a timely, caring, responsive fashion, I developed a far more loyal customer than before. Complaints are actually an opportunity to deepen customer service and allegiance.

We used this approach from the very beginning of Merry Maids. I wore a pager, and if a complaint came in, the receptionist would get in touch with me right away. Wherever I was, I would get back to that customer within minutes—sometimes within seconds—of his or her negative call. That was the first step.

The second step was that regardless of the nature of the complaint, I would always apologize right away. I would tell people the two most important words they wanted to hear: *I'm sorry*. I wasn't just saying it. I meant it. And I've found consistently over the years that that empathetic connection would go just about 95 percent of the way toward deflating the complaint. People felt that I cared. And I did.

Then, of course, I would work with them to come to a solution to the problem. Most complaints were pretty easy to handle. We came back and recleaned if something wasn't done right; we also worked hard to understand just what the client's expectations were. Often clients hadn't communicated their ideas about what they wanted. Once we had probed to find out just what it was they had in mind, then we could meet that need. And that made people feel that we really cared about them in a personal way.

So complaints are often an opportunity for increased two-way communication and, therefore, a strengthened relationship. If you handle complaints right, then that person will often turn into your best customer.

Certainly there were times that we received unjustified complaints, but for the most part, the concerns were about things that we could do better. And whether or not the customer was right, we would never argue.

Complaints also led to new ideas. It would have been negligent to turn away from those opportunities or to miss them because of defensiveness. Sometimes they pointed out bugs in our systems; we could use them to refine or streamline our business.

Speaking of getting the bugs out, one time a friend and I were at an Omaha restaurant. During our meal a cockroach crawled up on our table and stared at us as if we were on *his* turf. I called the waitress, assuming she would be horrified and get the manager, who would call pest control, tear up our bill, and apologize profusely.

Instead the waitress looked down at the cockroach, shrugged, and said, "Oh, those daggone things! They're all over the place!" She paused for a moment. "You guys need more coffee?"

Needless to say, we never ate there again!

Too many small business owners and staff get so preoccupied with their own experience that they forget the customers' experience. Or they get bogged down trying to prove themselves right in response to criticism or complaints. When you do that, you not only lose the customer (and the eleven people he or she will tell to never use your business), but also you lose the opportunity to refine your techniques.

Small business owners and entrepreneurs usually have strong egos—you have to in order to succeed. But you also need to know how to put your ego aside so that you can learn how to do things better.

We tried to do that at Merry Maids. We would get complaints not only from customers but also from our franchise owners. For example, early on in the business one of our Denver franchise owners told us that our window-cleaning products just were not working right.

At first we were defensive. Since our resource center sent out the cleaners in concentrated form and the various franchises constituted them by adding water, we thought it must be *their* fault. They must be mixing it up wrong.

Of course they told us they could read, thank you, and they were making the formula correctly. But the cleaner kept leaving streaks on customers' windows and glass-topped tables.

So we followed our own advice. "I'm sorry," I told the franchise owner. "Let me find out what's going on." And, yes, I discovered that the city-supplied tap water in Denver was much harder than our nice Omaha water, so we had to adjust our formula accordingly. We did, and all was well.

I can't tell you how many times our Merry Maids model was vastly enhanced because of customer or franchise owner concerns and suggestions. The home office was like an hour-glass. We would carefully consider suggestions, choose the best ones, and then disseminate them, refined and improved, to our franchise owners. In short, we were constantly perfecting our service because we were willing to accept the fact that it wasn't perfect to start with. We were willing to *use complaints* to make our business better.

Not one of us enjoys complaints or criticism. But whatever your field of endeavor, those who will succeed are those who thoughtfully examine criticism and then apply its wisdom to their lives. As human beings we all lose objectivity about ourselves and our projects pretty quickly. Other people's criticisms can be our best resource for improvements and insights.

In the service industry, most customers are more discriminating than ever. They know what they want. They are aware of options and choices. So in order to succeed, it's imperative that service providers *listen* to what customers want.

One of our key customer-service tools at Merry Maids was our comment card. After each cleaning the team members would leave a bright yellow postcard. It was stamped with the local office address so that customers could mail it in, or they could just fill it out and leave it for the following cleaning.

We asked for feedback regarding all the different areas of the home and for customers to rate our cleaning. We also asked for particulars and complaints—and here we learned a lot about our various customers' idiosyncrasies.

Of course, customers listed everything imaginable.

Some assumed that we were there not only to clean but to care for their animals. One Idaho woman wrote, "Calay [the cat] has been getting on the mantel with the plants, which he is not supposed to do. If he does that, he gets five minutes' *time out* in his bedroom. We think he is going through the kitty 'terrible twos.'"

And sometimes there were notes from the animals themselves, like this New Mexico dog: "Dear Merry Maids, would you let me out a few times while you're here? My backyard is fenced in, so I won't run away. I also would like a treat when I come in and maybe an extra one before you leave."

And then there were other unrelated requests:

"Could you please have the workers who are coming to my house today salt and pepper the roast in the Crock-Pot? I've got to be at work." And "before you leave, could you please take my turkey out of the fridge and put it in the oven at 375 degrees? It's ready to cook."

And some were simply mystifying: from a California couple, "We had two new kids last weekend, so look in the yard for them." Or, from an Ohio customer, "Throw away all the dishes and utensils currently in the dishwasher."

Other customers stuck to straight cleaning issues. For example, one customer noted that the maids hadn't vacuumed under Dad's chair. Dad evidently ate popcorn every night while he watched television. And so, from that point on, our maids were careful to glean every kernel he left behind!

Some people were sticklers about open windows' sills being wiped down. Others wanted beds made up in a certain way. Others wanted certain areas left completely alone. Others wanted the vacuum cleaner to leave diagonal patterns on the carpet, and still others wanted the toilet paper rolled under, rather than over. . . .

Preferences like these were easy to accommodate, and we

tried to meet any request within reason. When we did, we found that customer loyalty shot up accordingly. We would incorporate the comment cards onto each home's computer-generated worksheet for the day. In fact, this was a way to give some of the maids' management capacity directly over to the customer—and the customer was paying us to do it!

Our only problem was ensuring that our team members read the comments. Early on, I would run little tests. On the second or third line of specific customer instructions, I would insert a little incentive like, "I'll give you $5 if you read this!" I was shocked at how few maids collected from me.

So the word got out, first to our franchise owners, and they emphasized it to the maids: *Read the comments!* That was a key step to teach them the fact that the customer who feels that we are listening and that we are responsively serving his or her unique needs is a happy customer.

3. MASTER THE DETAILS

I have an acquaintance who schedules his business travel around Doubletree hotels. If there's a Doubletree in the city where he's scheduled to speak, he stays there. Why? Well, my friend says it's because of those two enormous, warm-from-the-oven chocolate-chip cookies that every guest receives as he or she checks into a Doubletree hotel.

Now, plenty of hotels provide nice service. They have restaurants and meeting rooms and clean towels and those little soaps and shampoos in the bathrooms. There's usually no particular reason to pick one over the other.

But only Doubletree does the cookie thing, and to my friend, and plenty of other customers as well, those warm cookies are a lot more than a sweet treat. They're a statement about the hotel's philosophy of customer service. They're *unique*. They're *personal*. And they smell like *home:* those long-ago memories most of us have of hot chocolate-chip cookies fresh from the oven. They make customers feel special.

Of course, it goes without saying that it's essential to do the big things right. In my business that meant providing customers with a clean home. But the secret to outclassing the competition lies in the details. As Doubletree shows, it's in the details that you can *surprise* the customer and in that surprise exceed his or her expectations.

At Merry Maids that meant that we didn't just clean to clean. We cleaned for show; that meant standard techniques that showed up in the details. We groomed the carpets, leaving nice, straight lines; we put a gold Merry Maids sticker on the toilet tissue roll. We put lemon oil on the shower doors so they wouldn't streak or spot. We sprayed cinnamon fragrance inside the front and back doors so that when the customer came home after a long day at the office, the first thing he or she would notice was the clean smell in the home, with the corresponding sense of sweet relief—"Ah . . . the Merry Maids were here!"

The way we dealt with details also said a lot about our corporate commitment to honesty: the team members would pile all the spare change they found in sofa cushions or wherever on the kitchen counter where they left their Merry Maids comment card. A small thing—few homeowners are going to care about the nickel and the penny that fell out of Dad's pocket while he snoozed on the sofa—but it spoke volumes about our integrity. Clients were trusting us in their homes; that little pile of change on the counter showed them that we merited their trust.

Often the team members found more than spare change. One New Jersey customer wrote, "Thank you for finding and returning my class ring I had lost several months ago. Without your honesty, I would no longer have my ring." Similarly, a woman in New York sent a note to the Merry Maids office: "Just a note to let you know I think the men you send to my house to clean are the finest. In particular, I want to acknowledge Garland. He found a diamond earring I had lost and brought it to me and asked, 'Did you lose this diamond?' Unheard of. All in all, you have a great crew!"

Another important detail was our method for cleaning floors. From the very beginning of Merry Maids, we always cleaned hardwood, tile, or vinyl floors on our hands and knees. Mops just move dirt around; in order to get that floor clean, you have to do it the old-fashioned way, even though it's really tough on your knees!

But when customers saw us cleaning that way, it was a powerful signal regarding our commitment to excellence. And although you might think that that posture was degrading to the team members, it was just the opposite. In our training we showed them that this was the most efficient method to get a floor truly clean, so they knew that they were doing it the best way possible.

And, of course, we provided them with knee pads, so they had the tools they needed to do the job with both excellence and comfort. Those yellow or green knee pads were just a detail, but they were a powerful symbol to both the client and the team member of Merry Maids' commitment to being the very best.

This business of mastering the details applies in *every*

arena of life. I could write an entire chapter on details, but here's the take-away point: If you want to excel in school or in business or in any area at all, first of all you must deliver an excellent product or performance. But to stand out from the crowd and rise to the very top, you must master the details.

The difference between good and great is in the details. I always felt it important to economize wherever possible but never to cut back on areas where the public sees your business, no matter how small. I always made sure, from the beginning, that Merry Maids' calling cards, stationery, logo, sales materials, and advertising were the very best quality I could afford.

Details create your public image, and like it or not, the first impression you make is the one that lasts.

The next element of superior service is closely aligned with attending to details.

4. PROVIDE SENSUAL SERVICE

Now that I've gotten your attention, this isn't quite what you might think it is. By sensual service I mean that you serve your customer in a way that appeals not just to the eye but to all five senses, if possible.

For example, those big, fat Doubletree cookies don't just *look* good. They *feel* good, warm and soft from the oven. They *smell* good: their chocolate aroma makes your mouth water. And, of course, they *taste* wonderful.

Nordstrom stores use the same approach. What does a tuxedoed pianist have to do with selling shoes and clothes? Nothing directly—and everything in terms of the appeal to the *ear* and the soothing yet festive environment that background music creates in their stores.

And that's the key. When you appeal to as many senses as possible, you create an environment where the customer feels special. That always involves the little element of surprise— exceeding expectations—that will keep the customer coming back to you.

So sensual service at Merry Maids meant a lot more than simply making a house look clean for the eye. Any good maid service can do that. As I've already mentioned, for us it meant making a house *smell* clean. As one Florida customer wrote: "I have been sick, so it was especially nice to come home to a well-cleaned apartment. The only downside is that I was too congested to smell the Merry Maids scent. I love that cinnamon smell!"

Sensual service also meant making the house *feel* clean— a customer could run his or her finger along a mantel or a picture frame or a bathtub edge and feel the absence of dust and grit.

This sense of domestic aesthetics became important to me when I was a young executive at Fairmont Foods.

Back in 1967 I became close friends with Art Dolken, the purchasing agent at Fairmont. I had just been transferred to the Terre Haute Fairmont plant. Glennis and the children had not yet moved, and I was living in a hotel for three months. Art and his wife, Nan, must have felt sorry for me; they were kind enough to have me over for dinner several nights a week.

Nan was a wonderful cook, and the way she presented the meals was as important to her as how the food tasted. I had grown up eating great food, but at my Norwegian childhood home everything was white: the fish, the potatoes, the milk, the plates, and the napkins. And with nine children, my mother didn't have a whole lot of time for artistic presentation. So meals were very good, but they were rather pale and bland.

So I loved the simple yet special way Nan Dolken would serve ordinary meals. She used brightly colored napkins folded in special ways or rolled in decorative rings. Her meals featured a lot of color, different shapes, and a variety of textures—bright vegetables, flowers on the table, velvety sauces, crisp salads.

The way she took just a little extra time to manage the details and make the meal appealing to the eye, the nose, and the palate really impressed me. I knew that that kind of careful presentation made the difference between the ordinary and the extraordinary, and I determined to incorporate that aesthetic care into whatever I pursued.

Here's a detail of how we did that at KAP's. Back in the mid-1970s, butter-flavored popcorn was a huge seller, especially at movie theaters. But you had to be careful: consumers wanted the butter sensation without too much heaviness. The corn couldn't be coated or greasy to the touch. So after some experimentation, I found that if we used just a little extra red food coloring in our formula, the popcorn came out a warm, rich yellow. It *looked* buttery. And customers loved it.

Interestingly enough, mastering aesthetic or sensual details can be infectious. When you do something ordinary with just a little extra panache, others will follow suit.

In one of the first homes Glennis and I owned, we had a small, nondescript yard just like everyone else's on our typical suburban street. I was somewhat compulsive about rooting absolutely every dandelion out of our lawn, and I also started mowing our grass on an angle, so you could see diagonal lines in the green. I'd seen that done on big lawns in upscale neighborhoods, and I liked the effect. Before long, first one neighbor, then another, and another started doing the same thing. And pretty soon our street had the nicest-looking lawns in the subdivision!

The Paradox of Profit

As you've gathered, mastering service, like the other principles of real success, boils down to some very simple precepts about human beings and their needs. As simple as they are, those precepts rest on inherent paradoxes: Financial returns come when we don't seek money as our primary goal. Lead by serving. Big success comes when you master little things.

The same type of paradox applies about the next principle of success—corporate planning. I didn't plan by looking at *today's* corporate spreadsheet or *yesterday's* profit margins. I didn't even focus on the numbers.

No, I would dream about *tomorrow*. And oddly enough, I would find that as I did, the numbers I wanted for *today* would follow.

CHAPTER 16

Principle Four

SEIZE TOMORROW:
Plan for Tomorrow's Market, Not Today's

Some years ago the movie *Dead Poets Society* brought the Latin phrase *carpe diem* back into common usage. In the film a whimsical English professor played by Robin Williams encourages a group of staid, upper-crust schoolboys to shed the constraints of convention and stop living according to their parents' expectations. "Carpe diem!—seize the day!" he exhorts them, encouraging them to fling off constraints and follow their dreams.

Carpe diem became a catchphrase. *Seize today!* College kids would toast one another with it in university pubs, meaning basically, "Eat, drink, and be merry, for tomorrow we die." For others the phrase meant a belligerent, winner-take-all strategy for living, a call to seize assets wherever one could. For still others it meant just take it easy one day at a time, the don't-worry-be-happy approach to life.

As I've thought about the principles of success, the phrase has come to mind. But real success, in both the business world and in one's personal affairs, isn't about seizing *today*—carpe diem. Today is too late. Success comes when we seize *tomorrow*.

Carpe Posterum

Carpe posterum, my layman's Latin translation of the principle of seizing tomorrow, is not some nasty internal medical exam. Seizing tomorrow is about being competitive in business and wise in life by making decisions according to *tomorrow's* market environment, not today's. That requires visionary planning, not just in the workplace but also in your family, your personal life and spiritual goals, your education, your church—every area of your life.

Now some elements of life and business just happen. But planning is not one of them. Here's the take-away point: Planning must be planned! You must schedule time, preferably away from the daily fray, to deliberately yet creatively assess where you've been, dream about where you would like to go, and figure out how to get there.

Unless you schedule time for aggressive planning, it won't get done. And if you don't look *ahead* to chart your course as a business—or a family, a ministry, or an individual—then you'll passively drift according to the winds and waves of the *moment*.

So I would like to isolate just a few helpful principles about planning. They are simple to execute, transferable to any business or undertaking, and in at least one respect radically—and I think refreshingly—different from most advice you'll read about business planning!

GET AWAY

The first thing you must do in order to plan well is get away.

For a family, that might mean a yearly trip to a special place, perhaps the beach or the mountains, in which every family member, including the kids, feels free to bring ideas, goals, hopes, dreams. It's good for individuals to get away as well. I know a lot of people who periodically go away alone for a mini-retreat to do personal planning and reflection.

Very early in the history of Merry Maids, we began to schedule at least two off-site planning sessions a year. This would include the members of our executive committee: Dale, Tom, Harlyn, and me. We would try to get away Thursday evening or Friday morning and then spend the rest of the weekend together. We would dress casually, eat well, sleep soundly, and generally use the planning time as a retreat away from the stresses and interruptions of the home office.

In the summertime we would most often go to our lake house at Norway Lake. For Dale and me, it was a great blessing to return to our family roots in order to plan how to grow bigger and stronger as a company.

And the lake relaxed all of us. There's something very restorative about the lapping of water against the shore. We had to get away from phones, interruptions, and the constant, jarring stress that we were so used to. We had to get where it was quiet so we could think creatively and really *listen* to one another.

Before our meeting Tom and I would assemble a good agenda. We wanted to make sure we could maximize our time together. Tom would always serve as secretary since he had a tremendous skill for taking impeccable notes and distilling our conversations into action points. I took on the role of moderator since I owned the company.

Situation Analysis

The first half day we would review the maid-service industry at large, our competitors, and the opportunities for Merry Maids.

1. REVIEW THE MARKET

It was important to start with industrywide, updated demographics. After all, Merry Maids began in response to my reading of the potentials revealed in relevant demographics in 1979; we continued to monitor those numbers as the years went by. We would look at the number of women in the workforce, dual-income family growth, and population growth by regions of the country.

Those numbers—which continued to rise each year—told us that we would continue to grow if we did things right. They also let us know where in the country we should concentrate new franchise sales efforts. We were careful to assess trends, to make sure the needs on which we were basing our business were ongoing directions for large numbers of people, not just isolated pockets of individuals.

2. REVIEW THE COMPETITION

Then we would review the growth or lack thereof of our next five competitors. Early on our number one competitor was The Maids of Omaha. We would discuss what they were doing and see if we could learn from their experiences. We were always surprised that they weren't growing faster because we knew the business potential was hot. But consistently, we were larger than the next five competitors combined.

I'm surprised at how many small businesses today don't take the time to examine their competition. We didn't do it to fixate obsessively on our rivals in the industry; we didn't want to make the mistake of letting our competitors, rather than our customers, drive our business. But we did find that taking the time to examine what the competition was doing was always a rich source of information and ideas—usually in terms of showing us what *not* to do. We saved time and money by learning from our competitors' mistakes.

For example, we would examine how other companies were advertising their businesses. At that time other companies were using franchise expos, but we saw that those arenas were a poor investment; they gobbled up a lot of time and produced mostly "tire-kickers" rather than serious prospective franchise buyers.

We also followed how other maid-service companies provided brightly painted company cars for their workers. Although those cars provided name recognition, insurance was very high for commercial vehicles, and we didn't see any real payoff for providing company-owned cars. So we chose to hire people who had their own cars, then we reimbursed them for mileage and provided them with magnetized Merry Maids signs.

Another important area of evaluation was how other companies paid their people. They compensated their workers at an hourly rate. We chose instead to compensate people with a percentage of the fee for each home they cleaned. That way a good worker could make more money based on his or her productivity, and it also instilled a sense of quality awareness. So over the years we found that our Merry Maids teammates were better compensated than the competition's workers and more motivated to work well.

3. REVIEW THE COMPANY

After looking at and learning from the competition, we would turn our sights toward Merry Maids. From the beginnings of these getaway planning meetings, our situation was always that Merry Maids was experiencing consistent, rapid growth. We would review the prior six months' reports and revenues and then ask probing questions: *Why* were we growing? Was it the quality and commitment of our franchise owners? Was it the training we gave them? Was it our marketing and advertising tools?

We would try to isolate the most significant contributor to our growth, particularly when we would compare the growth of each individual franchise operation on a year-to-year basis. It's important not to take growth for granted; if you don't know *why* you're doing well, you can't replicate and strengthen your success factors. Success can sometimes begin by fortuitous coincidence, but you don't want to leave it to chance or it won't last long.

4. BRAINSTORM ABOUT THE FUTURE

After analyzing the situation around us, the next planning step was deciding where we would devote most of our time. Using the knowledge we had already digested about cutting-edge demographics—i.e., where the needs would be in *tomorrow's* market—and what our competitors were and were not doing, and what the factors were of our own success, we would then shape those elements into future operating plans.

Like many businesses we would lay out one-, three-, and five-year plans. The shorter-term plans were detailed and definitive, the longer plans more big-picture, goal-oriented projections.

Well, everybody does that. Nothing new there.

But that's where our approach to planning got radical.

Because, aside from the projected numbers of franchises we expected to sell each year and an annual average growth rate in excess of 20 percent for our established owners, *there were no other numbers in our annual business plan.*

We believed that if we could help facilitate the success of our franchise owners, then the numbers would follow. Our plan always focused on practical ways we could help *people* succeed.

Grow your people, and your numbers will grow.

This focus on people rather than numbers flies in the face of conventional business wisdom. But as Merry Maids continued to grow and prosper over the years, I saw no reason to change our unconventional approach.

Of course we didn't *ignore* our profit margins; we would look for ways to cut costs and enhance profitability. But we didn't spend much time on the numbers. I've always felt that businesses that get wrapped around the axle on their numbers often lose their creative spark. Growth comes through helping people develop so their creativity can be unleashed—then the numbers you want will come.

As Merry Maids continued to grow, I realized that a lot of my unorthodox philosophy about numbers came from my experience at Fairmont Foods. At Fairmont we had spent hours poring over the past, hunting down who did what when, usually with people scrambling to cover their paper trails or to shift blame to someone else or to shift glory to themselves. I had told myself then that if I ever owned a business, I would not spend precious time haggling over expense details or worrying about the past. I saw too many people who were obsessed by past errors or misfortunes, and it robbed them of their creative energies. I resolved to learn from mistakes and look forward. I would try to focus on the company's *people,* and the *big picture.* Today Merry Maids continues to prosper, and Fairmont Foods no longer exists.

5. PUT IDEAS INTO ACTION

Some companies hold planning sessions, brainstorm about great ideas, and then get home and forget to implement their plans. Or, more often, their fresh new ideas get squeezed out by the sheer weight of busyness and precedent.

We made sure to go home and try our ideas. Here's an example:

As anyone in the franchise industry knows, communication between the home office and the businesses in the field is one of the most important company values to be developed. In order to stoke and strengthen relationships, you have to have reliable, easy communications systems in place. Otherwise, human nature being what it is, misunderstandings and strained feelings can develop—and you'll lose momentum as a business.

One of the ideas that came out of our first planning retreat was the formation of the Weekly Bulletin Board, which was a recorded message that became available every Friday afternoon; owners could call in on a special 800 number, at any time that was convenient to them, and hear me relaying Merry Maids news, tips, or developments. Sometimes the message might concern a timesaving tip a franchise owner had discovered, with kudos to the owner. This encouraged a creative environment in the field; owners were eager to share what had worked for them with their fellow franchise owners.

Other times the message might be about a new product or a marketing theme. Those messages were very simple and to the point, but their worth couldn't be measured. They created an environment of sharing and accessibility, a sense of connection to me and the company.

Today that phone bulletin board is of course obsolete. Now our messages go out via e-mail. The technology for transmitting the message has changed, but the principle has not: Communication to owners, in ways both large and small, is absolutely essential to good relationships, which in turn build success.

We didn't get those ideas in the hustle of the home office, however. We had to get away to a planning retreat—and then when we came back home, we put them into action.

6. ASSESS INDIVIDUAL NEEDS

During our planning meetings, we would also spend a lot of time looking at the track record and peculiarities of specific franchises and their owners. After all, no matter how well you codify your practices and your products, the service industry is not a science. Serving people in any arena is an art, subject to the wonderful, eccentric diversity of individual human beings. In our case, we had to keep the needs of our customers, our team members, and our franchise owners before us.

Our question was always, How can we help this particular franchise owner grow? How can we help move him or her from this current level of sales to the next level up? Helping owners in a stairstep series of incremental growth, with lots of recognition and affirmation at each new step achieved, kept success as an attainable goal for them.

And as they climbed those steps, they soon had translated small successes—like hitting $2,000 a week in sales—into big successes—like hitting $2 million a year in sales. As their self-confidence and success grew, so did our profit as the royalties came pouring in.

As we talked about individual owners, we would come up with very specific action items for each franchise. What about adding a second office assistant? What about targeting new neighborhoods in the area with a doorhanger campaign? Often we could see ways we could come alongside and assist franchise owners with ideas that they just didn't have the time or perspective to see on their own.

When those suggestions were given in the right spirit, they strengthened the feeling of family—all for one and one for all—that was at the heart of the Merry Maids corporate ethos.

We would also brainstorm about how to increase our media exposure. This was the arena of Tom Guy's genius. He understood the most basic premise of public relations. Newspaper and magazine editors and television news producers *have* to fill their space, day after day after day. They can't put out blank pages or empty airtime. If you provide them with timely, well-written human-interest stories about your business—tied to a timely hook—along with photo opportunities, you're doing them a favor.

Over the years we received millions of dollars' worth of free regional, national, and international coverage of Merry Maids because of Tom's expertise at giving members of the media what they needed—even when they didn't know they needed it!

Rules of Engagement

In our planning sessions, we worked according to several informal assumptions, or what we called rules of engagement. We promised to put aside our egos, be honest with each other, and then evaluate the results of the planning session at regular intervals.

1. THROW EGOS OVERBOARD

Fortunately, we usually met at a lake, so it was easy to toss personal control or self-focus overboard for the meeting. We would spend the first couple of hours as a transition time from the stresses of the office so that we could all get on the same wavelength. We would take a boat ride or walk on the beach to unwind. Then we felt free to brainstorm, come up with crazy ideas, critique one another's proposals, vent, and invent new scenarios—but without rancor or personal competition. After all, we were all on the same side, with the same goal: the increased success of Merry Maids. The success of the whole— the common good—was more important than one person's ego or bruised feelings.

So we had some very lively sessions. With the personalities of our particular leadership team, the dynamics would usually go something like this:

Tom would jump in with an opinion. Dale would say the opposite. Harlyn would say nothing. I would bring up a third point of view. And then we would all go at it. The fur would fly, and ideas would ricochet off the ceiling. We could become rather passionate because we all cared deeply about the company. Sometimes it was hard. But it was healthy—and in the end, our discussions would yield an outcome far better than any of us could have come up with on our own. We sharpened one another.

If a conversation on a particular point ended with a difference of opinion, I would make the final decision. And after that, we all unanimously supported it, regardless of differing opinions in the discussion.

That united front was very important when we returned to the home office and when we presented ideas to our franchise owners.

2. BE HONEST

Because egos had been tossed into the lake—at least for the duration of the planning meeting!—we didn't play games with one another. We could say what we really thought and get on with it.

3. EVALUATE

Once we had our list of things to be achieved and accomplished, the list provided the means to measure our performance. And after the planning session was over and we were back into the commotion at the office, the executive committee would evaluate the qualitative franchise sales and franchise growth on a quarterly basis.

Planning in the Office

When our executive committee needed to have short planning bursts before our regional meetings and the yearly Merry Maids national seminar, we would use the same planning principles I've just outlined. We would go into seclusion, away from the phones for two or three days, and script the meetings. We would examine every aspect of the time onstage, who would do what, and give people what they needed in order to succeed onstage.

We did not leave anything to chance. People knew what they were to say and when they needed to get offstage. That's not to say that we weren't creative and fun; but I have seen too many corporate meetings turn deadly—I'm sure you have, too—because of long-winded presentations from the front. Scripting made each person more succinctly comfortable with his or her part and made things move more efficiently.

The Benefit of Planning: More Face Time!

The net effect of concentrated periods of planning was that it meant we spent less time in meetings. As you can imagine, that was a win-win situation for everyone. We at the home office weren't tied up in conferences with each other, doodling on our coffee napkins, which meant that we were almost always *available* when franchise owners called—except when we were sequestered in our biannual or preseminar planning sessions.

Imagine that: a new franchise owner could call the home office, ask for me (or Dale or Tom or Harlyn) and have the radical result of actually getting me on the line. Not my voice mail. Not my assistant telling them that Mr. Peterson is in a meeting and will emerge some time next month. They got *me*.

That personal connection was a huge contributing factor to the sense of loyalty and excitement that created Merry Maids' success.

Work Smarter, Not Harder

In this chapter I've focused primarily on organizational planning. But at Merry Maids I also tried to create an environment in which each person had a strong sense of *personal* direction and fulfillment that comes from keeping one's priorities in order. Planning is the first step in creating efficiency in one's home life, business, church and volunteer activities, and other responsibilities. I found that when I had things planned properly, my sense of direction became much clearer, and I was able to keep my priorities straight. I tried to pass that on to others.

Most prospective franchise owners came to us because they wanted to have a better life. They wanted more time for themselves and time with their families.

As I talked with our new franchise owners over the years, it seemed to me that many Americans felt as if their lives were out of control. Corporate executives were threatened by downsizing. Middle managers were frustrated by lack of company loyalty. Professionals such as teachers, dentists, and lawyers didn't like the changes sweeping through their professions.

But they all came to Merry Maids with one overriding common feeling: a lack of control, both over their future plans and their daily lives. So for most of our new owners, owning their own business represented a way to take control, to run their own shop, to create their own hours, to design their own future.

The Merry Maids franchise owners who used our principles and persevered ended up enjoying great financial success as well as the great luxury of free time that success can bring.

But getting to that point was very, very tough, with plenty of frustrations, long hours, and a myriad of competing responsibilities.

When I would talk with stressed-out owners, I could relate to what they were feeling. I would tell them what worked for me.

1. REMEMBER YOUR PRIORITIES

I always carried an index card with me, stuck in my jacket or my shirt pocket. On it were my few big-picture goals. "Maintain a happy marriage." "Spend time with kids and grandchildren." "Achieve financial independence." Those are huge goals, but they are achieved by means of everyday choices and decisions. Everyone's list will be different, but for me, just the reminder of that card jostling in my pocket would help me assess how I was spending my time. It took discipline, but I would drop any little activity that didn't lead toward my big goals.

2. DELEGATE

All business owners and entrepreneurs have a tendency to try to do everything themselves. I remember one regional seminar we held in Minneapolis; we conducted a time-study review of what each owner did in a typical workday. Most were shocked when they saw how much time they spent doing tasks that easily could have been delegated to someone else. Most of them were spending between 60 and 70 percent of their time performing nonessential activities.

I was an offender too. For example, it took me a long time to give up opening every piece of mail that was addressed to me. Bobbi, my wonderful assistant, finally started wrestling the mail away and hiding it until I got over my compulsion. And, of course, I found that if I concentrated on doing only those things that only I could do, I had much more time to devote to the big picture, to make sure that we were moving toward our key goals as a company. If I as the leader had my head down, focused on too many details, the whole organization would get off track.

3. EAT A FROG A DAY

Maybe you are familiar with the saying "Eat a live frog first thing every morning, and you can be pretty sure that nothing worse will happen to you for the rest of the day!" We all deal with tasks that are pretty unappetizing, and, like most people, I would procrastinate in accomplishing the things I didn't want to do. Day after day certain items would languish at the very bottom of my to-do list. Finally I realized I just had to put the dreaded items at the top of the list and force myself to do them first. It was like eating a frog. But it was also amazing how good it felt to get those things done and out of the way. It energized me for the rest of the day.

4. DO ONE THING AT A TIME

Today's culture tells us that we should be doing any number of things at the same time: make cell phone calls while driving, get your stock quotes or your car insurance while you get dressed; learn Portuguese while you're on the treadmill, e-mail your mother. Even watching one television channel at a time is now passé. We've got to have a split screen going while we surf the hundreds of available cable channels.

Some people claim that multitasking makes for efficient time management. Maybe I'm old-fashioned, but I think all it really does is increase stress and impair relationships. I encouraged our franchise owners: just do one thing at a time.

Many times I needed to shut down various activities so that I could concentrate on one thing at a time. I would schedule occasional quiet times with my office door shut in order to catch up on phone calls or take some time to do some creative thinking.

5. DISCIPLINE YOUR HOURS

A recent survey of the CEOs of America's fastest-growing privately held companies showed that 41 percent work at least sixty hours a week. Certainly entrepreneurs work long hours—in part because their businesses demand it, in part because they need the rush, in part because they love what they do.

At Merry Maids, I put in very long hours until I began to realize that I could work smarter, not harder. I began to take three-day weekends during the summer months. I would go up to the lake house; I might have a big pile of work with me, but my physical absence from the home office was therapeutic, and the staff could contact me if they needed me.

I discovered that my absence did not affect sales, profits, growth, or employee morale one whit. We continued to grow 40 to 50 percent each year. I realized that when I worked long hours, I would often become preoccupied with the day-to-day details that were better handled by someone else.

I remember a boss who told me many years ago, after I had been complaining of working long hours, "Dallen, some people can do a job in eight hours, and others take a little longer." From that I learned that working longer hours isn't necessarily more productive. If we're disciplined about focusing our energies where they should go, we'll find we just don't need to spend quite as long at the office each day. And that is very good for the priorities of marriage and family!

One of Merry Maids' top owners, Tom Paul of Aurora, Colorado, is a classic example of work discipline. He's always in the office early, which is the most important part of a Merry Maids owner's day. That's when you've got the whole team together before they go out to clean, and it's up to you to set a successful, positive tone for the day.

But Tom takes off early several days a week, and he schedules sales calls for only one evening per week. (Many owners do sales calls whenever they're asked to come out.)

Tom keeps his priorities in order. He puts his family commitments on his work calendar and blocks off time to be home with his wife, Jodi, and their two daughters. His desk is clean, his employees emulate his attitude, and his customers' homes are sparkling.

For Tom, small business ownership *has* been the route to escape the stresses of the corporate rat race.

Dare to Dream

So planning and the purposeful structure of one's time can be great liberators for the individual. And to return to the corporate level, they can also liberate a company's creative potential. Careful planning doesn't stifle creativity; it unleashes it.

At Merry Maids our planning was focused on people—how to help them succeed. We didn't noodle our numbers to death. We weren't looking over our shoulder to see who was trying to get our job. We were looking at our current success in the marketplace and discerning how to take the elements of that success into tomorrow's market. That took vision, creativity, and courage.

Our planning took place in the context of a lively environment in which everyone was committed to working very hard, of course, but we were having fun while we were doing it.

I see too many companies and organizations today that have lost the fun. They've stifled the creative environment that open-ended planning can create.

I've seen too many board meetings dominated by Power-Point presentations from nervous number crunchers showing just how lovely the company's bottom line looked over the prior six months. Too often those numbers have been massaged so they're not even an accurate reflection of what really went on.

Companies expend huge amounts of time creating glossy reports to make board members or stockholders feel happy and comfortable so the meeting can end and everyone can go back to managing the status quo. Mistakes or viable challenges are buried and never discussed. Corporate denial sets in.

That's how companies can go soft and lose their edge.

Plan to Take Hard Risks

I remember one Prison Fellowship board meeting in which we were discussing the pilot project for what became the Inner-Change Freedom Initiative.

It was a risky proposal: an invitation for Prison Fellowship to actually take over a wing of a Texas prison and run it according to Christian principles. (The state would still provide the security and administration, but PF would run the programming.)

I listened to the discussion. Some people felt that it was too risky. They listed all the problems, the scary numbers, the obstacles. The potential for gain was huge, they agreed, but so was the potential for disaster.

At that point I leaned forward at the conference table.

"You know," I said, "if I had listened to my accountants and attorneys and the naysayers, there never would have been a Merry Maids."

In some ways my comment was a turning point. The board

decided to move forward, and Prison Fellowship went on to set up the InnerChange program. Yes, it presented huge challenges. It stretched the staff and management in creative and painful ways.

And it has been an incredible success! The state of Texas, with enthusiastic support from Governor George W. Bush, has invited Prison Fellowship to run not just *part* of the prison where InnerChange began, but the *whole institution.*

The change in the inmates' lives has been tremendous; other states, seeing this real rehabilitation—when every conventional method of rehabilitation has failed—are clamoring for the InnerChange program to come to them. As I write, we've already established new sites in Iowa and Kansas, with more planned.

All that to say that sometimes companies and organizations can lose the boldness that established them in the first place. They can take on an attitude of protecting the status quo and playing it safe. Too often, there's a fear of rocking the boat—but then the boat ends up dead in the water.

In order to grow and maintain your vigor, you have to learn from the past. And you have to be willing to take on new challenges. That means new risks, with the potential for failures and difficult experiences.

But I've seen over the years that it is precisely in times of difficulty, loss, or error that we have the opportunity to learn the most. If companies—and individuals—choose to do so, they can profit greatly from adversity.

And that's my next, rather unlikely, principle of real success: *Pain!*

Principle
Five

EMBRACE PAIN:
Adversity Can Teach and
Strengthen You

I've conducted an informal poll; you can try it too. Ask ten of
your friends about their worst nightmare. Most will talk about
violent death or the loss of a loved one—but once you get past
those elemental fears, the everyday foreboding my friends
mentioned most was the fear of failure.

For all kinds of reasons—the blow to pride, financial loss,
death of a dream—we all dread any threat to success.

But I've found over the years that failure can be an important preparation for success. Whatever enterprise we're in—
whether it's a small business, a long corporate career, or an
ambitious school project—failure can teach us lessons we
would learn no other way. Of course, we don't seek failure or
pain! But if we live long enough, it will come.

I was forty-two when I encountered my first daunting
defeat.

I told you in chapter 6 about the most notable business failure I've enjoyed—when KAP's started heading down the tubes.

When KAP's Went Kaput

When KAP's began to slide, its failure was primarily the result of matters that I could not change. No matter what I did or how much expertise or money I threw at the problem confronting me, I just could not control the wild surge of oil prices in 1978 and 1979. I also couldn't do a whole lot about potato crops and skyrocketing costs.

So my costs of production were much higher than they had been; as a result, my profit margins were thinner than a Lay's potato chip. Speaking of Lay's, that was the other problem that was clearly outside my control. As a regional company, we just didn't have the size or flexibility to compete with the giants of the industry like Frito-Lay.

We could slash our prices, but we weren't in the business as a charitable enterprise. We were just too small; we couldn't ride it out.

I've always liked the simple wisdom of this well-known prayer: "God grant me the serenity to accept the things I cannot change, courage to change the things I can, and wisdom to know the difference."

So having accepted the things I could not change, we were, by God's grace, able to sell KAP's.

What Did I Learn?

Never again would I embark on a regional or local business. I wanted to be national. I also knew that I did not want to be caught in the middle again. I wanted a business with low overhead.

By this I mean that at KAP's we were stuck between sky-rocketing supply costs and a market that would not bear corresponding price hikes. Consumers just weren't going to pay any more than $.69 for a bag of potato chips, regardless of how much it cost us to make them.

With Merry Maids our product was service. The only supplies we needed to make that service happen were vacuum cleaners, rags, and a few simple cleaning concoctions.

I also learned that I would not go into a business partnership again. Dick Kerns and I are still close friends; but even though I'm highly relational, I discovered that in terms of business ownership, I needed to have sole responsibility. The buck needed to stop at my desk.

It was very difficult for Dick and me to lay off our KAP's employees, all of whom had become friends. But many of our workers were young, and they had gained good experience at KAP's. All of them, including the various ex-prisoners we had employed, were able to find other jobs.

Those are just a few of the very clear practical lessons that came with the demise of KAP's.

FORCED TO DREAM

But the loss of KAP's also cleared the way for me to think creatively and aggressively about the future. I never would have done that if I were still busy running our snack company.

But when I was forced to dream, I dreamed up Merry Maids.

I would never have voluntarily chosen for KAP's to fail. No one chooses defeat or pain of any kind.

But without adversity, we can get too comfortable—and we don't tend to grow or seek change while we're comfortable. Without the failure of KAP's, which was disconcerting and wrenching at the time, I never would have had the wisdom or practical experience to grow the huge success of Merry Maids, which far exceeds anything KAP's could ever have become.

DEEP PAIN

Now there are different kinds of pain. Business failure is one thing. Human loss is another. As I've been writing this book, I've lost my father, a friend to violent crime, and a sister-in-law to a car crash.

Those losses have been terrible. Yet I feel very thankful that I have not, as of yet, had to deal with life's most difficult pains—the death of a spouse, the loss of a child, the terrible kinds of suffering that we see on the news all the time. As I write, yet another American high school has become the scene of unspeakable violence. I cannot imagine the depth of suffering those students and parents feel. Certainly I don't feel qualified to speak to those deep degrees of loss.

But all of us, in various degrees and in different ways, *will* encounter adversity and pain in this life. And adversity, no matter how "superficial" or how harrowing, always presents a choice. If we choose to deal with it and learn through it, pain can strengthen us greatly. As the Bible puts it, "God disciplines us for our good. . . . No discipline seems pleasant at the time, but painful. Later on, however, it produces a harvest of righteousness and peace for those who have been trained by it" (Heb. 12:10-11, NIV).

In my experience, adversity and failure in the business arena have been key parts of success. In most endeavors, the sure way to grow is through pain; if you learn its lessons, it can take you to the next level of achievement.

That's also true spiritually, in relationships with those you love, and in your dealings with the world at large.

So we don't look for adversity. But we can embrace it when it comes.

I realize that in saying this, I'm bucking much of the conventional wisdom of the world around us.

ESCAPE?

Check out the self-help aisles at your local bookstore, and you'll find shelves full of books giving very different advice about adversity, like this:

When you start to feel like a rabbit in a leghold trap, escape. If your home feels like a prison with no way out, escape. Escape from a dull and boring routine that's slowly but surely killing your spirit. . . . Find a way out. However you must, escape from the constant needling of people who live their lives under a perpetual storm cloud. Get away for an hour or two, for a month or three. If you must, leave the marriage. Or the country. If you must, leave everything behind. When you've served your time and are ready for freedom, pardon yourself, and then escape.[5]

[5] Rachel Snyder, *365 Words of Well-Being for Women* (Chicago: Contemporary Books, 1997), 106.

Books with exhortations like this are a response to a huge demand in the market: people are *desperate* for help to deal with the difficulties and disasters of life.

But many of the authors out there won't help much. As in the quotation above, some will tell you that when problems come, you should escape at any cost. Others encourage you to deny the existence of negative situations through the power of your self-will. New Age gurus like Deepak Chopra command a huge audience; Chopra will tell you to see coincidences as events orchestrated for your "SynchroDestiny": meditate long enough, and you can follow your *dharma* as a participant in a consciousness-created universe: "Things may go wrong, but *they don't bother you anymore.*"[6]

That would be nice. You can get the same result with a bottle of booze.

No, there's no easy out. Much as we would love to escape, repress, or redefine painful problems, they are an inescapable part of life. We can't control the problems, but we can address our reactions to them.

So the question must be, then, how will we *choose* to deal with crises when they come? Will we accept them for the growth they can bring? Or will we allow pain to defeat and embitter us?

The Choice Is Up to Us

Our modern word for *crisis* comes from the Greek *krisis,* which literally means choice or a time for decision.

Fortune 500 consultant Roger Crawford has built a successful career in spite of a huge challenge: He was born

6 Deepak Chopra, "SynchroDestiny," *New Age* (March/April 1999): 60, italics added.

with just one leg and severely deformed hands. Roger's determination in the face of his handicap propelled him to play high school football and college tennis; he became the first physically handicapped player to be certified as a teaching professional by the U.S. Professional Tennis Association. When Roger spoke at a Merry Maids national seminar some years ago, we were all struck by his tenacity, humor, and faith.

Roger possesses hard-won insights about adversity; he now tours the country telling businesspeople that rebounding from adversity requires one key element: resilience.

In his book *How High Can You Bounce?* Roger says,

> [We] have a conscious choice. We can allow ourselves to freeze up, calcify, to slowly become brittle and inflexible like frail old trees waiting to blow down in the next strong wind. Or we can take steps to develop and maintain our resilience. Fortunately, resilience is a skill you can learn. . . . If you're alive, you're going to face challenges and hardships.
>
> We can't control which difficulties we'll encounter, but we can control how we'll respond to them. We can *choose* to be victims or victors, winners or whiners, optimistic or pessimistic.[7]

I agree.

Let me give you a pretty searing example of the power of choice, a very difficult blow that came during the early days of Merry Maids.

---

[7] Roger Crawford, *How High Can You Bounce?* (New York: Bantam, 1998), 2–3.

Family Matters

As you know, Merry Maids was a family undertaking. As we grew and sold more franchises, more and more family members came on board. Our daughter Kim and her husband, Pete, were with us nearly from the beginning. So was our daughter Kris and later, her husband, George.

Pete became my right-hand man; George managed the Omaha company-owned Merry Maids franchise.

In August of 1982, Merry Maids had fifty-five franchises. We were working hard, as always, but in a lot of ways we had hit our stride and were growing well. We had ironed out a lot of the bugs and streamlined our operations.

So it came as quite a shock when I discovered that Pete and George wanted to leave Merry Maids and start their own maid-service company. A friend told me what they had been talking about, and I went to them.

"If you want to leave," I told them, "you might as well do it right away. Go ahead."

And they did.

Using the practices we had established at Merry Maids, Pete and George started a maid-service company called Daisy Fresh. They replicated Merry Maids' systems, forms, techniques—just about everything we had worked so hard to develop.

Fortunately we were working so hard that we didn't have a lot of time to let their betrayal eat away at us. But the tension was horrible. Kim and Kris, of course, were in an extremely awkward position, and we all felt varying degrees of tension, anger, division, betrayal, and pain.

Remember that *crisis* means choice, a time for decision.

When George and Pete left, I looked at the choices before me. I could react in anger and pride, close off communication, and close down the relationships. After all, I could have claimed that *I* was in the right. *I* had been a nice guy. *They* were the ones causing the rift.

RIGHT?

Well, the problem is that "being right" at all costs usually costs the relationship. If I had taken that route, we would probably still be estranged. The rift would have worsened over the years.

I thought about it. I knew that I wasn't the easiest father-in-law in the world; maybe these guys needed to try their wings on their own. I had to be willing to examine my own part in the problem and to look at my character—had *I* been proud or difficult? Where was *I* at fault?

I knew that anger and division would accomplish nothing but hurt everyone, especially my daughters.

So I chose to let go of the anger.

That didn't mean that the relationships were fixed instantly in some nice, tidy solution. It meant that I had to be willing to let the whole thing heal over time.

That took patience—which is always a good lesson to learn, but one that we rarely seek. (Maybe you've heard the old prayer, "Oh, Lord, please grant me patience. And I want it *now!*")

As it happened, Daisy Fresh was in financial trouble within months. I loaned Pete and George money to make payroll one time, but I could see that things were falling apart. My sons-in-law had thought it would be easier than it really was.

Soon they parted ways. Pete started yet another maid-service company. This one was called Spring Clean.

Several months later, George asked to meet Glennis and me at a local Mexican restaurant. He broke down and wept, and told us how sorry he was for the pain he had caused. He asked if we could forgive him—and, of course, we told him we could. I helped him find a buyer for Daisy Fresh, and a year later George came back to Merry Maids, working in franchise sales. (Eventually he went on to other business ventures; years later, he and Kris were divorced.)

The relationship with Pete was healed as well. Even though he and Kim divorced in 1984, we still maintain a relationship with Pete. He calls me whenever he faces a major decision in his current business, and we shoot ideas back and forth.

For me, in that family fracas, the short-term challenge of reconciliation was far better than the long-term damage of division. But the responsibility—and opportunity—lay with me, in how I *chose to respond* to the difficulties those relationships posed.

Thorny and unwelcome as that problem was, it brought opportunities for growth and strength. Pain and adversity always offer that potential.

Looking Back

I think earlier generations knew more about adversity and the character traits that it can build than we do today.

Our forefathers came to America in search of religious freedom. They braved incredible opposition and suffering, and persevered with good humor through situations that would baffle and defeat us today.

These heroes are not dusty figures from a history book. These were real men and women, just like us. And they endured pain to establish a country where they could live free, where character and conviction could create a great nation.

Similarly, my parents' generation knew the challenges of self-sacrifice and tough times. My mom and dad were married in 1933 in the depths of the Great Depression. My mother was recently cleaning out one of my dad's closets after his death, and she found a receipt he had kept in a box for sixty-five years. It was a sales slip from their honeymoon. They had stayed in a cabin in a small town about fifty miles south of New London, Minnesota, and had cooked their meals there. The grocery slip showed they had bought two pork chops for $.05; the total bill was $1.33. They honeymooned for a week for less than $20.

My parents had a strong sense of sacrifice, humility, and integrity. I never heard my dad say anything negative about anyone. If the conversation was heading that way, he would change its course and say something positive about the person. He instilled in us a sense of doing the very best we could, then leaving it at that, not worrying about the outcome. I can still hear my dad's voice saying, "Ah, that's good enough." It's a comforting thought.

My parents knew how to scrimp and save and help their neighbors through tough times. Because of the difficulties they faced, they knew how to endure, how to sacrifice for others. And they always had hope: they looked ahead to a brighter future for their children.

And they achieved it. They, and the entire generation who shared their values, passed them on to those of us who followed. The World War II generation also passed on a country brimming with opportunity.

As a result, people like Glennis and me grew up with a strong sense that we could achieve success if we worked hard. We had hope.

What is hope? Not just a vague wish that something might turn out the way we want it. For example, when we started Merry Maids, we didn't just have an earnest aspiration that some big company would come along and buy us for millions someday.

No, my hope for our success was built on the long hours and hard work that Glennis and our kids and I put into it. Hope springs from the belief that today's sacrifices and today's acts of duty and faithfulness will eventually bring tomorrow's success.

Hope is about hanging in there during the *process*. But what I find today is that many young people in the upcoming generation know little of the process of hard work. Perhaps because of their familiarity with instant technology, they assume they'll enjoy instant gratification in whatever they attempt.

Looking Ahead: The Challenge

It's ironic: Through hard work, Glennis and I have been able to provide for our children and grandchildren beyond our wildest dreams. The very prosperity we have worked so hard to achieve has created an atmosphere that has protected them from any kind of economic hardship.

We're like so many other parents I know. The human tendency for all of us is to make it easy for the kids, to protect them from pain or discomfort at all costs.

But the cost could be their character.

So—and here I am speaking to my peers—I believe that we who have been blessed materially must be very careful not just to check out and enjoy our retirement. And we cannot afford to be too materially indulgent with those we love.

My concern is that when life is too soft and easy, people can become soft as well. And then they don't have the strong backbone to be tough when the challenges do come, as they inevitably will.

So in our will, for example, I've made clear stipulations for our nineteen grandchildren. Any money they receive after we are gone is tied to responsibility; they cannot receive it if they are not gainfully employed. They won't need to work for the *income* it brings, but I believe they'll need to work for the *character* that hard work and adversity can bring. We love them too much to let them have it too easy!

In short, we must teach those who follow us so that they will have a sense of the legacy they inherit here in America and a sense of the strong character we must recapture, the character that is won through effort and pain.

As we'll see in the next two chapters, that's a tremendous challenge—and opportunity—in the unprecedented times of flux and change that are upon us.

CHAPTER 18

Principle Six

CELEBRATE CHANGE:
Technology Is Your Tool,
Not Your Master

The most succinct description of the twentieth century would be to say that change has been the constant. This era of incredible technological development has ushered in more changes more quickly than in any other time in human history.

And in all my years of working closely with thousands of human beings, I couldn't help but notice that people don't exactly embrace change. When we would introduce a new system, technology, or product at Merry Maids, I don't care how wonderful it was or how much time it could save franchise owners, there was always a groan throughout the company until people grudgingly got used to the change.

Similarly, even though Glennis and I are pretty easygoing types, change was hard on our kids and us. During the years I worked with Fairmont Foods, our family moved six times.

Moving meant new homes, new schools, new neighbors, and new churches. No matter how great they all were, moving was always tough.

Embracing change just doesn't come naturally to most human beings. It's a *learned* behavior.

But it's a necessary one: Looking ahead, I see little reason to suppose that technological, geopolitical, environmental, and economic changes will slow down at all. It's clear to me that the men and women who succeed will be those who anticipate and celebrate the accelerated patterns of change that characterize modern life.

When I think of the changes that have come in just my lifetime—technological advances and political upheaval my grandparents could not have imagined—I'm overwhelmed.

I remember back in 1984, when Glennis and I spent a week in Eastern Europe. We were part of a church tour following the steps and life of Martin Luther. In Leipzig, which was considered to be the cultural center of East Germany, we nearly choked on the thick clouds of burning coal smoke that shrouded the dark city. I yearned for color, for flowers, for green grass, for some expression of warmth, hospitality, or creativity. But the city, with its massive, deteriorating apartment blocks, was like a prison—a fitting monument to totalitarian suppression of the human spirit.

Our tour guide, Helga, was a study in contrasts. She was a member of the Communist party—otherwise she wouldn't have been allowed access to us—but she was deeply intrigued with America's capitalistic culture. She was an atheist, yet she knew the Bible better than many Christians I know and was conversant with the details of Martin Luther's life and ministry.

We ended our tour in East Berlin. On our last night there, Glennis and I ventured out after dinner. Walking the dark streets of that dismal city, I stared up at the Berlin Wall. I thought about the Iron Curtain, the labor camps, and the evil grip of totalitarianism on so many millions of human lives. East German guards paced the perimeter of the wall—and I thought about how many people had lost their lives at that very place, trying to scale the wall in a desperate, futile dash for freedom.

The next morning we said good-bye to Helga. I gave her a hug—which surprised her to no end—and told her how much I hoped she might one day visit us in America. Her gray eyes clouded.

"Oh," she said, "how I wish that could be . . . but it is impossible. It will never happen."

Who could have anticipated it? Just five years later, the Berlin Wall came tumbling down; one by one the entrenched communist regimes of Eastern Europe and the Soviet Union crumbled altogether. The collapse of communism, perpetuated by men and women of unwavering commitment to the power of the human spirit, was the most astonishing and dramatic whole-scale change of our century. Sometimes I still can't believe it really happened!

We see change not only on a grand scale but also in our own lives. As I've told you, I was born in a rural farmhouse. My siblings and I walked two and one-half miles to a one-room country schoolhouse.

Today there's not a single country school left in the state of Minnesota. When I tell my grandchildren about my early years, they look at me as if I just beamed in from another planet.

The medical profession is another field that has experienced great change. A good friend, Dr. Kathy Bliese, operated a very successful medical practice in Omaha for many years. Then in 1997 she and her partners sold their clinic to a large corporation—and a year later her position was eliminated in a corporate downsizing.

Since then Kathy has made a complete career change because of the turmoil in the medical profession. When her company was bought, the new management expected her to see an average of six patients an hour. Kathy felt that she could not begin to administer the relational, human dynamic of her profession in just ten minutes with a patient!

The stock market is another area of dramatic change. Within just a few more years, stockbrokers as we know them will be obsolete. More and more people are buying and selling equities directly over the Internet. Its instant access is one of the major factors in the Dow's great climb over recent years.

The average investor now has access to the same information formerly available only to brokers. I remember just a few years ago when the first thing I would turn to every morning in the *Wall Street Journal* were the stock quote pages; that was the only means I had to check on my investments.

Today that medium is like ancient history. The same information is available with instant updates via the Net. The same obsolescence will apply to travel agents and any other type of sales broker.

The ATM card as we know it will soon be history as well. You can now get cash through a machine just by opening your eye, with the camera recognizing your iris. Even identical twins can't fool this technology. (Dale and I have tried!)

Soon television will be totally different. Family rooms will have high-quality pictures on flat screens hung on the wall— and through our computers we will have available choices that we can't even imagine today.

And, of course, typewriters are long gone. Soon computer keyboards will be as well. For parts of this book, I used software that allowed me to talk to my trusty PC; it obligingly created the text of what I said, taking my accent and speaking habits into account. All I had to do was print it out!

On another front, I've noticed change in employee loyalty. During my business career I worked for three companies: Fairmont, KAP's, and Merry Maids. Today's college graduates will have an average of thirteen different employers during their working lives. They will average around three and one-half years on each job.

That means that training will be a constant in most businesses. Factories will turn increasingly to robots that will work twenty-four hours a day, remain loyal to their employer, give the employer no grief, and never leave for a better job!

Because of this, as well as the sophistication of communications technology, there will be more entrepreneurs in the future. And because of labor shortages, they will be forced to use inexperienced employees. They will find that these employees won't have the same vested attitude toward the company as they do, so it will be even more challenging to be the very best and at the same time be innovative.

The service industry is changing as well. When we started Merry Maids in 1979, we were a novelty. There was no other nationally franchised maid-service business. Housecleaning companies were primarily local mom-and-pop operations.

Today there are a number of national cleaning companies, and as I profiled in chapter 14, today's homeowners are far more likely than they used to be to use *all* kinds of home services: housecleaning, lawn care, pest control, security systems, window cleaning, meal delivery, carpet-cleaning, vets who will spay your dog in their mobile clinic parked right in front of your house. You name it.

Domestic demographic trends—like the number of women in the workplace and the number of two-income families—were ripe to make Merry Maids a success in the early 1980s. Those trends have continued. In fact, they've intensified, so I think just about any service industry that can deliver excellent, timely help for today's busy families will be guaranteed success.

(My coauthor, Ellen Vaughn, has an eight-year-old daughter and five-year-old twins. She told me the other day that if someone out there would just come up with an in-home laundry and sock-matching business, there is no limit to the amount of money she and people like her would be willing to pay for that kind of service!)

And since the economy has been strong during recent years, many consumers have more disposable income to spend on services and other goods.

I see no reason to believe that the strong economy will change in the next few years. And I know that men and women with a strong work ethic, creativity, and the ability to embrace change can find their niche for business success.

The New Demographics

Finding those niches lies, as always, in understanding today's changing trends that will dictate tomorrow's market needs.

Just consider the needs of today's emerging demographic groups.

Women. Women influence or control 80 percent of all buying decisions. They handle 75 percent of American families' finances and spend two of every three medical dollars. In dual-income families, 22 percent of wives out-earn their husbands today, compared to 4.4 percent in 1970. (Interestingly, working women who out-earn their husbands still shoulder most of the household duties, such as cooking, cleaning, shopping, and paying bills.)

Seniors. I'll talk more about this in a moment, but tomorrow's products and services will need to be designed for consumers' aging physical capabilities. Creators of products and services will also need to keep an important psychological factor in mind, and that is the need for seniors to retain their independence as much as possible.

Generation X. These members of our population, born between the mid-1960s and the late 1970s, typically like risks, challenges, and innovation. But they are often difficult to manage and organize since they reject conformity, authority, and structured systems.

Generation Y. This huge group, made up of the 88 million young people who follow Generation X, has never known life without the Internet. They will demand interactive consumer opportunities. The services that meet their needs will do very well as the Net Gen comes into more and more economic success.

The New Affluents. This smaller but influential sector of the population has the money to spend on services. They are typically in their midforties, in good health, and earn more than

$200,000 a year. They want what they want, when they want it, how they want it. They refuse to wait in line for anything. They use personal shoppers, in-home delivery of services from groceries to pet care to massages, manicures, and pedicures. They provide their children with nannies; music, dance, and riding lessons; sports clinics; and summer camps.

What Everybody Wants

As diverse as all these groups are, they have a few basic needs and wants in common. First, they want choices—and so the entrepreneurs and service providers who succeed will be those who offer *options*.

CHOICE

When I first started Merry Maids, we were a 100 percent cash business. Customers, typically out of the home and off at work, would leave us a check on their kitchen counters.

But today's customers would never be content with only one option. They pay with credit cards, ATM direct-debit cards, and soon will be using money cards, smart cards, and virtual digital cash on the Internet. Smart businesspeople will take advantage of any new developments that make it easier for the customer.

The sports-apparel industry gives a good example of offering customers options. When I was young, the only athletic shoes worn by most Americans were tennis shoes. The only choice, really, was whether you wanted high tops or low tops, black or white.

Today the market has become so diversified that we have specialty shoes tailored for just about every sport: running, walking, aerobics, biking, walking the dog, whatever. And today's celebrity-driven world of professional sports has upped the ante to far more than shoes, with athletes from Tiger Woods to Michael Jordan to Ekaterina Gordeeva marketing everything from shoes to clothes to fragrances to hamburgers.

Overall spending on sports and health-related items has skyrocketed in recent years. That fervor has led to a search for new experiences on every front, like the trend of "extreme sports," such as skydiving, stunt driving, heliskiing, and ever-increasing numbers of clients willing to shell out $65,000 for the death-defying thrill of climbing Mt. Everest. Corporate sponsors like AT&T and Nike compete to invent the most daring new sports and to back extreme sporting events. Adventure travel is now a $200 billion industry in the U.S. and $3.4 trillion worldwide, growing 9 percent a year.

SERVICE

I've profiled excellence in service in chapter 15, but it's worth mentioning here in the context of change. Ironically, when consumers are busier and more demanding than ever and when technological advances *could* enhance service greatly, many companies have lost the *human touch*.

Technology is a tool, not a master. But some companies allow their wonderful technological tools to cause them to forget their reason for being: the customer!

We've all sat at the telephone trying to contact a company or a service, and we've seethed in frustration, lost in the labyrinth of voice mail—one of the worst inventions on the planet, in my opinion.

Certainly voice mail can be a useful tool for leaving messages, but it is primarily used as a convenience for the company. However, it is a convenience that comes at the expense of the customer's well-being, and I find it particularly appalling in the service industry. *"Just get me a human being!"* I want to scream sometimes after waiting through six different menus with twelve various options—when all I want is an answer to a simple question.

I feel that same loss of the human component with directory assistance. I want an operator! I don't want to listen to the recorded message of some hired Hollywood voice! I don't want to talk to a machine!

Similarly, e-mail is great, but I fear for the day when we all sit at our computers all day—never speaking, never smiling, just clattering the keys of cyberspace, using digital cash, shopping at virtual malls, connected to one another only by the tenuous ties of the World Wide Web.

Now, in spite of these comments, please understand that I am a great fan and user of technological advances—*if* they are truly advances. That means they must both sharpen efficiency *and* enhance the human element, the relational factor of any business. I heard recently of a company whose leader had instituted a "no-meeting" policy. Across the board, company employees were to communicate via e-mail and telecommunications connections. That meant that colleagues whose cubicles were next door couldn't just stand up and ask each other a question. No, they had to use e-mail. This high-tech policy backfired: rather than streamlining efficiency, it ended up decimating morale and costing the company millions in lost profits.

Of course, technology does make possible quick human connections that would not otherwise exist. At Merry Maids most of our franchise owners, scattered all over the world, are able to instantly communicate with one another via the Internet. Owners experiencing a particular type of business problem can communicate with peers who have already dealt with the area in question and who can offer quick, experienced solutions.

But in many cases, advances in technology (like fancy phone systems) have caused companies to forget the plain basics: timely, responsible service!

In this kind of environment, any service provider who promises and delivers *on-time* service that not only meets but also *exceeds* the customer's expectation can have a heyday in the marketplace.

FLEXIBILITY

In today's atmosphere of flux, it almost goes without saying that we must be flexible. We must adapt to market changes.

For example, it is understandable that Woolworth's, the old small-town American institution established in 1879, went under in the late 1990s. The old five-and-dime stores were a staple of my growing-up years. But you can't get much for a nickel or a dime any more, and huge chains like Target and Wal-Mart—not to mention grocery stores that now offer everything from prescription drugs to flip-flops—took over Woolworth's more limited market.

So the last Woolworth's closed in 1997, and the corporation now has a new name—the Venator Group. Venator has become the industry leader in the lucrative sport-shoe and apparel market. Woolworth's realized that in order to survive, their company had to be bold and adapt to the environment around them by changing directions—and they were willing to eradicate one of the best known names in American business to do so. Smart move.

I think a lot of large bookstore chains have showed similar adaptability. Many people predicted that the advent of amazon.com and other book-buying opportunities on the Internet would make bookstores obsolete. But as you've probably noticed, the big chains like Barnes and Noble or Borders seem to be doing well.

Why?

They've transformed their stores into modern-day coffeehouses. They've put in coffee bars and pastry cases, overstuffed armchairs and listening stations, even working fireplaces.

Sure, people can order books over the Net. But many people today are hungry for a sense of community. And you can't meet a friend for cappuccino, or curl up with a new book next to a warm fire, on the Internet.

Looking Ahead: A Model Opportunity!

As I've already mentioned, one of the booming markets on the American scene today—and one that will only grow exponentially over the next century—is the field of senior care.

In the last ten years, the number of Americans eighty-five years old or over has increased by 42 percent. Americans age eighty and older are the fastest-growing group of people in the U.S. today, increasing at a rate of more than 16,000 a month. In just thirty years, the number of Americans age sixty-five and older will grow to 70 million—that's a 106 percent increase from 1996. By 2050, one person in five, or 20 percent of the U.S. population, will be sixty-five or older—compared to just 7.5 percent in 1996.

Significantly, huge proportions of today's seniors also have the disposable income in retirement to get what they want. The increase in wealth holdings has accelerated greatly with the rapid growth in the equity market, allowing American seniors to live far more comfortably than at any other time in history. And because women tend to live longer than their spouses do, most of the seniors with significant wealth holdings are women.

So, as you can sense, if I were looking for something new to launch—and believe me, I'm not—I would jump into the field of senior care, primarily targeted toward women.

I've never met an elderly person who was in a nursing home by choice. In-home senior care offers a tremendous alternative today. And it is often less costly, as it is vastly more comforting, than traditional nursing homes.

That's why Paul Hogan's business is booming.

One Friend's Story

I first met Paul Hogan in 1985. He was a college student at the University of Nebraska, majoring in finance, and Paul had heard me when I had taught a class for the franchise study program. He was interested enough in Merry Maids to apply for a spot in our internship program; one Saturday he came to my office for an interview.

I was interviewing several candidates that morning, but Paul stood out. He made a great first impression—he was impeccably dressed. And as we talked, I could see that he was very enthusiastic and eager to learn. To me, those are just about the most important qualities for business success. I felt a real kinship with Paul. He seemed very clear about his goals and very purposeful about how he conducted his life. I knew he had great potential.

After Paul graduated, he came on board full time with Merry Maids. He coordinated our company information flow, feeding information to our executive committee. Then he moved to franchise support and marketing. Then from 1988 to 1994 he served as our franchise sales manager, using his immense people skills to help Merry Maids' sales continue to soar.

In October 1989, soon after we had moved to Minnesota in the wake of the Merry Maids sale, I returned to Omaha to make a luncheon speech at the chamber of commerce. I hadn't anticipated that members of the media would be there, but a number of reporters attended the event. During the question-and-answer period afterward, I was asked about business opportunities of the future. I spoke from the top of my head about something I believed deep in my gut. I said that if I were to start a new business, it would be in the field of senior care.

Well, the front page of that evening's edition of the *Omaha World Herald* included a headline that read something like "Merry Maids Founder Has a Better Idea."

Lots of people read that article about my comments on senior care—including Paul Hogan. He clipped it and started a file.

And in his spare time over the next few years, Paul researched carefully, reading as much as he could about the growing presence of seniors in the U.S. Whenever he traveled, he would check the local Yellow Pages in an unofficial survey to see what kind of senior-care options existed. There weren't many.

Also, as Paul talked with customers in the course of his Merry Maids job, he surmised that the elderly clients seemed the least satisfied. Not because their homes weren't getting cleaned properly, but because they wanted more time and attention than the team members were able to give.

In short, they needed *companionship*. If someone was in their home once a week, they wanted to be able to sit and talk with that person, to share a cup of tea. A worker who was paid according to how many houses he or she cleaned just couldn't spend that kind of time at one house.

Paul thought about seniors' needs and services that weren't already being met by existing franchises: things like light housekeeping, meal preparation, and transportation for trips to the doctor, the grocery store, or the hairdresser.

Meanwhile, Paul's ninety-seven-year-old grandmother was living with his mother. Paul saw how his mother and her siblings were willing to go to any lengths to avoid nursing-home care for their mother. And needless to say, Paul's grandmother had no interest in leaving home.

When Paul looked into national demographics, he saw a clear need for a company to come along and help bear the caregiving burden of countless families like his own.

Paul and his wife, Lori, started compiling a list of names, much as Glennis and I had done when we were dreaming up Merry Maids. One morning Paul woke just after dawn with the name Home Instead clearly in his mind. It evoked what his company would be all about: a viable *alternative* to the nursing-home care seniors wanted desperately to avoid.

Paul continued to research and refine his idea while he saved his money. Then, when he had $22,000 in cash, he borrowed $18,000, held his breath, and took the plunge. It was a big risk—he was thirty-one years old, had a wife and three kids, and was leaving a secure, well-paying job. I told him, "Franchising can be one step ahead of starvation," and Paul responded, "Sounds great. I need the challenge."

Paul and Lori started Home Instead Senior Care out of his mother's home. His grandmother was in on the action from the start; later, when it came time to interview potential caregivers, Paul would watch how they interacted with his grandmother before they sat down with him for their interview. Their rapport with Grandma—or lack thereof—was the best barometer of their suitability for the job.

Paul says that he learned from Tom Guy and me about the importance of his marketing materials. He knew that his initial brochures would create the public perception of his business. And he wanted that image to be an impression of where he was *going*, not where he *was* in those first wobbly weeks. So he spent the time and money to develop first-class letterhead, brochures, business cards—the works.

Then he sent letters and brochures to his family and friends. He and Lori took different areas in Omaha and each visited nursing homes, home health-care companies, bank-trust officers, anyone who was in a position to refer elderly people in need of help to Home Instead.

(Today that model in Paul's business is called the "four impression" program. Franchise owners are trained to develop relationships with those who can refer clients, since 80 percent of their business will come via that avenue. They schedule an initial meeting with, say, a nursing-home director. A week later they might drop by with a small gift for the person as a thank-you for his or her time. The following week they stop by again, this time with a magazine article or a newspaper clipping related to geriatric issues. The fourth time it might be an invitation to lunch or coffee. The point is, Paul knows that the service industry is about developing relationships, which grow through reinforcement. Franchise owners must genuinely care about their customers, their workers, and the people who are in a position to send business their way. Paul's system works!)

Next, Paul and Lori interviewed potential caregivers. At first they focused on people near their own age, the types of able-bodied service workers Paul was used to hiring at Merry Maids. Then, as he learned what the market had to tell him, he discovered that the ideal caregivers were women in their fifties. They could relate to the elderly clients better: for example, they could remember the same presidents, and they didn't think the New Deal was a game show. They also had greater empathy and patience—they knew that in just fifteen or twenty years, they would be in need of help themselves.

Then came Paul and Lori's first few clients—but he needed to grow beyond three customers.

Like me, Paul believed that if his idea could work in Omaha, it could work anywhere. And like me, Paul had a large and supportive family. His brother John was watching what was happening and wanted to be part of it. Within a few months John moved back to Omaha to take over management of the Omaha operation so Paul could concentrate on developing his disclosure statement, his training program, and other systems within the company so his service could be replicated. Two fraternity brothers also got interested. They and Lori's uncle were the first to purchase Home Instead franchises.

In an industry where three out of four new franchise ideas fail in their first year, Paul is going gangbusters today, with hundreds of franchises across the country.

Paul says one element that sent his growth skyrocketing was media coverage. Just as at Merry Maids, that came through Tom Guy's principles at work. Guided by Tom, Paul didn't spend a lot of money initially to jump into television, radio, or newspaper advertising. He knew that successful public relations is not about slick campaigns; it's about relationships.

So Paul set out to develop friendships with members of the media. Every month he would go to local journalists with news releases, quick human-interest stories about Home Instead's impact on the local community—and editors, hungry for good copy, would print them.

Eventually, through this ongoing contact, members of the media got used to thinking of Home Instead Senior Care as the expert in the industry—and editors and reporters started regularly calling Paul.

The key to PR, just as with every other aspect of the business, was cultivating *relationships*. Paul says he learned that at Merry Maids; he's also sought to be as personally involved as he can be with the staff, franchise owners, and potential buyers. When an inquiry about a franchise comes in, Paul gets on the phone. People realize that they've gone straight to the top and are talking with the founder and owner, not an assistant three people removed. That personal touch invests Home Instead with a strongly relational focus.

When Paul's new franchise owners come to town for training, he makes a point of spending one-on-one time with them. "That five-day period is really the one opportunity I have with them to set the course for our entire relationship," he says. "So I invest time in them. Nobody's too old, too new, too big, or too small to listen to. I want them to leave our training program with confidence in us—and confidence in themselves."

Paul must be succeeding in that goal: nearly one-third of his new franchise owners are referrals from existing owners.

Although Paul certainly hasn't encountered much failure at Home Instead, he has been quite open to the lessons that adversity and challenge can teach. He says his number one challenge has been to properly define, confine, and communicate his business identity.

For in senior care, as in most other service businesses, it would be very easy to lose your focus. Paul says that he's had to be careful to hold to his convictions rather than follow the advice of professional consultants (or all the naysayers who discourage any gutsy move forward).

He's had to stick to his guns and stay true to his company identity—while being bold enough to brainstorm about ways Home Instead *can* expand to provide more creative services for the growing senior market.

I've included Paul's story as a conclusion to this chapter for a number of reasons.

First, Paul embraced change. He looked at the changing demographics of American society, perceived a hole in the market, and met the need.

Second, I am thrilled at Paul's success. I've known him since he was in college. Both Tom Guy and I have mentored Paul, just as others mentored us when we were young.

And third, Paul's story shows how the success principles that I've outlined in this book are not unique to me. My success at Merry Maids wasn't a fluke or a lucky break.

As Paul's story shows thus far, if you apply the principles of real success, you'll achieve it.

But I would be remiss if I left the principles of success at just the six we've examined so far.

For there is one more tenet necessary for real, lasting success. I hope it will be the case for Paul and others like him— even as I pray that I will continue to apply it as well!

Principle Seven

STAY TRUE

I see the next two decades as a time of great excitement and hope. Of course I'm an optimist, but I do believe that the closing years of my life will be witness to widespread creativity and success in many different arenas.

For one, I believe the economy will remain strong. Unemployment continues to hold at a low rate—even though twenty-five years ago people were concerned that computers and the technology age would take jobs away from human beings. That has not happened.

I also believe that the Dow will top 20,000 within the next five to ten years, and 30,000 within two decades. Certainly there will be periods of fluctuation, but I think the net result will be a period of wealth that we have never before experienced in this nation—and an even more immense divide between rich and poor.

That concerns me.

As you know, I believe that hard work and core values like self-sacrifice, duty, and faith are integral to individual character. They are the basis of our moral strength as a nation as well. If we lose those foundations, our continuing prosperity is for nothing. The ash heap of history is full of rich but corrupt nations that lost their moral authority and fell into decline.

For both nations and individuals, affluence satisfies down deep and long term *only* if it is used to help others. For Glennis and me, the greatest joys over the last twenty years have had nothing to do with our wealth and everything to do with how we've been able to use money to bring joy to others—from prisoners to students to inner-city kids to friends to our family. Those riches last forever, regardless of market fluctuations or business upheavals.

That is very simple. But it's the core of real success: Stay true to eternal truths in the midst of these changing times, and you will do well. Love God, love others, and you will have peace.

I thought of that last spring when I walked the cornfields of the homestead where I was born. My father had just died at eighty-seven. He had lived a long, good life.

I passed the old garage where Dad had been working on his latest invention—a boat lift that won't ever get a patent, but its creative challenge kept my dad's mind sharp to the end.

I looked up at the brick farmhouse where he and my mother had lived for sixty-four years of marriage. They'd had their tough times. They raised nine children. And they both endured, faithful to the end.

I looked down the hill toward the lake where we had fished and skated and laughed with friends over the years, and then up toward the high, white steeple of the roadside chapel my dad built in 1987. He had wanted a place for the people of the countryside to worship near their homes, and he had painstakingly built the little church with his own funds.

When I looked around and saw the lasting evidences of my father's character, I saw the deep satisfaction of a life well lived. I saw abiding commitments to God, family, and friends. And I thought, *If I can pass that legacy on to others as my dad passed it on to me, I will have succeeded.*

Stay true.

With
Gratitude

I never intended to write a book. It came about only because
of the encouragement of family and friends, and particularly
because of the insistent urging of my friend Bill Pollard, chairman and CEO of ServiceMaster. For years he told me, "Dallen,
you should write a book." Then he'd ask me every time we saw
one another, "Well, Dallen, how's it coming?" Now that it's
completed, I extend my sincere thanks to Bill for his persistence!

I also have so many wonderful family members and friends
to thank. As you've read, each of our five children played a key
role in the early days of Merry Maids' growth. Our two youngest, Karma and Brett, were the first to pitch in. Our second
daughter, Kris, was the voice of Merry Maids early on. Kim, our
oldest daughter, took a big risk to move back to Omaha and
help us in those early days; our oldest son, Brian, and his dear
wife, Kim, also moved back home to help us at a critical period
in Merry Maids' growth. I can never thank our kids enough for
their sacrificial love and help!

Tom Guy, my longtime friend, professional partner, and
advisor, gave of his expertise even before we opened our doors.

His commitment to perfection always made me look better than I was. This book is richer because of his willingness to write, critique, and encourage.

My brother Dale gave me the unique insight and perspective that only a twin could give! I could always depend on Dale for candid, excellent counsel.

Chuck Colson has been a friend and confidant for many years; without his insight and knowledge about the writing process, I might have given up. I am deeply indebted to him for his caring, loving, and indomitable spirit!

Ellen Vaughn is the most capable writer I have ever known. Her patience, expertise, and loving persuasion allowed this book to become a reality. Simply said, without her this would have never been written.

And above all, I am deeply grateful to my dear wife, Glennis. For over forty years Glennis has been faithful, loving, critical when I didn't seek it, humbling when I didn't want it, but always caring, as only she could be, to keep me focused. I thank God for giving her to me!

Dallen Peterson
Naples, Florida
March 29, 2000

Appendix A

25 STEPS TO A SUCCESSFUL SMALL BUSINESS

These steps reflect a number of the principles I've fleshed out elsewhere in this book. But here they are in digestible nuggets so that you can refer to them easily and reap their benefits. Although some of them concern franchising in particular, their concepts apply for any small business enterprise.

1. COMMUNICATE WELL

As a franchiser, you must have strong oral and written communications skills. Use them often. The time it takes to make a phone call or write a note will be multiplied many times over in its relational value with your franchise owners.

2. COMMUNICATE CREATIVELY

Use a variety of tactics—whatever works—from weekly bulletin boards to e-mails to monthly mailings to bimonthly newsletters, to quarterly teammate newsletters, to videotapes.

3. TREAT FRANCHISE OWNERS AS YOUR GUESTS

Always reach for the tab, send them flowers, go the extra mile. They will feel they are getting something back for the royalty they pay you.

4. SURVEY YOUR FRANCHISE OWNERS

Do this at least once a year. You will find out what they're thinking, and their insights will give you planning tools you never would have realized on your own.

5. CONDUCT AT LEAST TWO PLANNING MEETINGS A YEAR

Take your planning team out of the office, away from phones and other distractions. Review what you've accomplished and chart where you need to go.

6. ANTICIPATE, RATHER THAN REACT TO, CHANGE

Research demographics and read extensively about upcoming trends. Prepare your business for tomorrow today.

7. USE DISCIPLINE IN YOUR BUSINESS MEETINGS

Stick to your agenda, and start and end on time. Human nature being what it is, meetings can extend indefinitely if you let them. But a meeting that drags on drags everyone down.

8. DON'T SET EARLY PRECEDENTS

If you create expectations among your franchise owners, you may have to continue practices that are not cost effective and produce questionable return. For example, early on Merry Maids started lavish incentive trips for owners who produced well. These cost lots of money, and the return on our investment was sometimes questionable. But once we had started them, people expected them.

9. SELL ONLY SINGLE FRANCHISE TERRITORIES

Multifranchise territories rarely produce the same sales volume that a single territory produces. People tend to reach a certain comfort level and rarely take their additional territories to the same sales level as their primary one.

10. KEEP INTERNAL POLITICS OUT OF THE CORPORATE OFFICE

Make every employee feel important, and treat home-office staff with the same courtesy and priority that you do franchise owners.

11. MAINTAIN RECORDS OF EVERY CONTACT WITH FRANCHISE OWNERS

Phone logs are very simple to keep—and they will protect and help you should you run into disputes or misunderstandings with owners.

12. EMPLOY A LIVE HUMAN BEING TO ANSWER YOUR PHONE

I realize that voice mail is the convenience of the decade, but it is rude and inconvenient for your customers and owners. Service companies cannot afford to use an automated phone-answering system. Make sure you have a warm, professional receptionist who can meet the needs of those who call.

13. REMEMBER THE MEDIA

Newspapers, magazines, television news programs all need you. They have pages and airtime to fill every single day, and if you give them well-written press releases and human-interest story ideas, they will use them—and you'll get free publicity.

14. CREATE A GREAT FIRST IMPRESSION

Lead your staff in dressing well and maintaining an orderly, professional home-office atmosphere. Once a week buy a big bouquet of fresh flowers for your reception area, and it will be a warm, inviting, positive place for both your staff and visitors.

15. FORM AN EXECUTIVE COMMITTEE
Use the executive committee for important decisions, and make it the scapegoat for unpopular ones.

16. GIVE YOUR FIRST FEW FRANCHISES AWAY, IF NECESSARY
While this may sound like a foolish thing to do, it really is quite sound. You need experience before you can grow, and a satisfied first franchise owner will lead you to other new owners. Plus everyone wants to be part of something that already has momentum. At Merry Maids we numbered our very first franchise #101 just to give a feeling that things were already well under way.

17. KEEP YOUR RECEIVABLES CURRENT
Never let past-due royalty fees run over thirty days. You need that disciplined cash flow to provide the quality and service your franchise owners need and expect.

18. USE REGIONAL COORDINATORS INSTEAD OF AN ADVISORY COUNCIL
Most franchise companies have an advisory council that is elected by the franchise owners themselves. Merry Maids has opted to use regional coordinators who are appointed by the home office at the beginning of each year for a one-year term. (Many serve multiple terms.) We found that appointing the coordinators ourselves allows us to have more control and connection with people in leadership, rather than leaving the choice up to franchise owners.

19. DON'T PUT DOWN YOUR COMPETITION

Potential franchise buyers would often ask me about other
maid-service companies. I would encourage them to check
out the others. I never said anything negative about the competition, even when I was aware of problems. I felt there was nothing to gain by criticism; if we were a superior company (which I
believed we were), then the careful buyer would end up with us.

20. IDENTIFY YOUR STRONGEST FRANCHISE OWNERS, AND GIVE THEM JOBS TO DO

People like to be recognized, and they enjoy helping others.
Our mentoring system in Merry Maids came at very little cost
to us, but it provided invaluable training through having
strong franchise owners help newer ones.

21. REMEMBER YOUR TWO CUSTOMER GROUPS

Your franchise owners come first, but serving their clients with
excellence is what will make you successful.

22. MAINTAIN UNIFORMITY

Your franchise owners may want to reinvent your wheel.
Don't let them do that. Insist on conformity to your hard-
won systems and operations throughout the company.

23. CREATE A RESOURCE SUPPLY CENTER FOR ALL YOUR PRODUCTS

A resource center not only makes your franchise owners
dependent on you, but it also strengthens your relationship
with them since they cannot get quality supplies cheaper anywhere else.

24. NEVER UNDERESTIMATE YOUR FRANCHISE OWNERS

Properly encouraged and motivated, your franchise owners

will set the milestones for what can be accomplished, beyond what you might have imagined.

25. KEEP THINGS FUN!

If you're having fun, your staff and franchise owners will as well. Don't allow business crises, problems, or frustrations to rob your joy. Celebrate small milestones. Have pizzas delivered for no reason. Set aside a day every spring when everyone wears sunglasses to work, and take lots of photographs. Sponsor contests. Everyone works better in a positive atmosphere—just use your imagination as you create yours!

Appendix B

FOR MORE INFORMATION ABOUT MERRY MAIDS AND SERVICEMASTER:

call 1-800-WESERVE,
or *visit their Web sites* at **merrymaids.com** and
servicemaster.com

TO FIND OUT MORE ABOUT PRISON FELLOWSHIP AND ITS MINISTRIES IN YOUR AREA:

write to

Prison Fellowship
P.O. Box 17500
Washington, D.C. 20041-0500

or *call* 1-800-497-0122
or *visit their Web site* at **www.pfm.org**

About the Authors

Dallen Peterson is the founder and retired chairman of Merry Maids, the nation's largest housecleaning service, which was acquired by ServiceMaster in 1988. Dallen serves on many philanthropic and educational boards, both locally and nationally, including the Board of Directors, Prison Fellowship Ministries; the Board of Directors for the ServiceMaster company; the Board of Regents, Waldorf College; and the Board of Trustees, Luther Seminary. Dallen has been active in community and political affairs as well as with prison ministries for many years. He and his wife, Glennis, live in Naples, Florida.

Ellen Vaughn is an award-winning author and speaker. Her novels include *The Strand* and *Gideon's Torch* (coauthored with Chuck Colson). She collaborated with Colson on seven other nonfiction books, including *The Body, Kingdoms in Conflict,* and *Against the Night.* Former vice president of executive communications for Prison Fellowship Ministries, Vaughn has also written for a number of publications, including the *Dallas Morning News, Christianity Today,* and *World.* She speaks frequently at

Christian gatherings and retreats and has been featured at writers' conferences in the U.S. and Canada. A native of Washington, D.C., Vaughn holds a Bachelor of Arts from the University of Richmond and a Master of Arts in English literature from Georgetown University. She and her husband, Lee, live in Virginia with daughter Emily and twins Walker and Haley.